② ③

The third house occupied by James Toplis's successors (among them William Daniel Harding) as 'James Toplis & Son, Auctioneers, Appraisers and Surveyors, & to the Sun Fire Office' certainly by 1845 and until 1890, was No. 16, which is the large house above, with (in 1822) the royal coat of arms over the door.

IN THE WAKE OF DISASTER

*200 years of The Toplis and
Harding Group*

IN THE WAKE OF DISASTER

200 years of The Toplis and Harding Group

DAVID WAINWRIGHT

QUILLER PRESS
London

First published 1990
by Quiller Press Limited
46 Lillie Road
London SW6 1TN

© David Wainwright and
Toplis and Harding 1990

ISBN 1 870948 29 7

Designed by Hugh Tempest-Radford Book Producers
Printed in Great Britain by Southampton Book Company Ltd

Contents

SWIFTNESS FIDELITY VIGILANCE AND

Introduction

IN 1990, Toplis and Harding – assuredly one of the largest firms of loss adjusters in the world – celebrates its 200th anniversary.

Two hundred years after James Toplis began work in the City of London as an upholder, his name is still familiar in the City, and far beyond it. No doubt he would be very surprised. Yet having enjoyed more years on earth than most of his contemporaries (he lived to be 85) and having seen his young protégé William Daniel Harding take the firm into still more profitable and successful times, James Toplis had good reason to suppose that he had started something substantial and enduring.

He began work in troubled times. Europe was in fever. A year earlier the French Revolution had taken place, leading to considerable worries in Britain that similar disruptions might cross the Channel. A few years later Napoleon came to power, and for two decades Britain was at war.

Two hundred years later, the greater Europe is again in political fever. And not only are the political problems still unsure and challenging; the insurance claims resulting from climatic change and industrial misjudgements are proportionately no less. In 1989 there were four major disasters. Hurricane Hugo caused damage of at least $4 billion. The San Francisco earthquake provided claims of almost $1 billion. The spillage of oil from the tanker *Exxon Valdez* resulted in claims of more than $500 million, and the Phillips Petroleum refinery fire in Texas led to claims of over $1 billion. All this was in the year following one of the most terrifying of disasters, the fire on the Piper Alpha platform in the North Sea, which led to claims of $1.5 billion. Indeed, as this book went to press, Britain was being ravaged by further storms leading to still greater damage, and claims against insurers.

Not all the work of loss adjusters, as the successors of James Toplis have become in the twentieth century, is concerned with disaster. Much is ordinary plodding investigation, establishing (in survey work) what might happen, and what the accurate proportions of risk may be; other work is concerned with making agreements between parties of differing opinions. So the loss adjuster has to be well blessed with common sense, and with a strong sense of fairness.

The skill of loss adjusting has only in this century been formalized. In the nineteenth century those who did the job were called 'assessors'. In the days when James Toplis began, their work was done by the 'upholders'. This story, therefore, is not only the account of one firm: it reflects the development of a profession.

1. The Upholders

IN THE late eighteenth century the City of London was becoming increasingly prosperous as a financial and business centre. But it was still a domestic place where tradesmen lived mainly 'over the shop'. For this reason, the trade of 'upholder' was an important one. The name means 'upholsterer' and is linked with the soft furnishings that need stuffing to support or 'uphold' them. The founding ordinances of the Worshipful Company of Upholders, incorporated in 1474, specified feather-beds, pillows, mattresses, cushions, quilts, curtains and 'sparvers', or bed-canopies. Many upholders naturally extended their business to deal in furniture and clothing.

When a rich man died in the London of 1790, his posthumous affairs would be dealt with by the parson, the lawyer, and the upholder. The upholder was originally the undertaker, supplying the upholstered coffin. The duties of the parson and the lawyer were defined by their professional codes. But there are many jobs, small and great, that need to be done on and after such occasions; and these fell to the upholder. He would dispose of the deceased's effects, often by auction; he would clear the house; and he would often sell the house also. His skills therefore often spread into what would today be called surveying, appraising, valuation, auctioneering, and estate agency. Those who followed this trade developed whichever aspects of it were most profitable. Some expanded their businesses into furniture manufacture, some into surveying, some into estate agency, and some (among them Toplis and Harding) into insurance valuation.

It was in 1790 that the name of James Toplis of Lamb Street, Spitalfields, first appeared in the books of the Upholders' Company. His father, Harvey Toplis, a warehouseman, had recognized that 'upholding' was a promising and expanding trade, and had paid 100 guineas (around £6000 by 1990 values) for his son's apprenticeship. James Toplis worked well, and soon became a Freeman of the Worshipful Company of Upholders, giving his address as 9 Old Broad Street, in the City of London.

1

James Toplis.

Indeed, after a few years he was confident enough in his prosperity to marry. His wife's name was Mary Hedges and she lived in the City in the parish of St Mary Magdalen, Milk Street. They married at St George's Church, Middlesex, in the summer of 1801. (James Toplis appeared personally before the London Diocesan Registrar on 9 May 1801, and he signed the application for a marriage licence in a good firm hand, with some artistic flourishes.)

In the eighteenth century, fire was a constant hazard in the crowded streets of the City, which had learnt little from the Great Fire a century earlier – except that now the buildings were no longer of wood, but mainly of brick and stone. There was a growing business in insurance, where one of the leading companies was the Sun Fire Office. Intermittently during the eighteenth century the Sun employed surveyors of buildings and of stock; there were some years

James Toplis's signature on his marriage notification (London Diocesan Registry).

when this arrangement was terminated, and special sub-committees of the Board were set up to survey particular risks. By 1773 the Committee of Management of the Sun Fire Office decided that they must, after all, employ a Surveyor of Buildings and Surveyors of Stock, on a part-time basis.

The Committee of Management kept a wary eye on this system, never apparently entirely satisfied that the Office was getting value

3

for money from its part-time employees. In 1808 they set up a Committee of Enquiry into the work of the surveyors, and on the Surveyors of Stock came to the conclusion that

> the Salary attached to each (being £150 p. annum [around £10,000 p.a. at 1990 prices]) is fully adequate and is a handsome compensation for their general labours. The salary [is] proper for the office. The credit of holding the office is . . . to be duly considered. The Duties . . . vary according to circumstances, being at the time very laborious, and requiring all the attention of these officers, while at other times they have little or nothing to do.
>
> At no time does the Business of the Office occupy more than a portion of the exertions of these Gentlemen, as each of them . . . carries on a private business, which their respectability of character, their talents, industry, and introduction from the Appointments they hold under this Office, have rendered very considerable, tho' not perhaps equally so.

However, the doubts of the Committee of Management were confirmed when a few years later they were faced with a little local difficulty. One of the surveyors, Mr Collard, had gone to appraise the results of a fire at Mr Glover's, hatter, in St James's Street, on 22 November 1810. On 12 November Mr Collard reported to the Town Insurers' Committee of the Sun that Mr Glover's loss was £140.11s. and presented this for settlement.

The Committee asked Collard what salvage would be recovered for damaged hats and brass plates. Mr Collard said that unfortunately so far he had not recovered anything, 'not having been able to find purchasers for either of the above articles'. The Sun Committee, smelling a rat (or singed hats and melted-down brass plates), adjourned the matter until their next meeting.

Meanwhile the energetic Secretary of the Sun Fire Office, Phillip Bewicke, did a little detective work. When the Committee next met, on Boxing Day 1810, Collard told them that he had obtained an offer of £10 for the salvaged hats, and that he had sold the brass plates for 8d. a lb to be melted down. Unfortunately for him, Bewicke had discovered (and presented written evidence) that Collard had sold the brass plates – five days before the earlier meeting – to a Mr Parker, plumber and glazier, for 6½d. per lb, which sum, added Bewicke pointedly, 'has never been accounted for to the Sun Fire Office'. The Committee decided that Mr Collard deserved to be dismissed, 'that an Office, so important in itself, may be filled by a more zealous and trustworthy servant.'

On 7 February 1811 James Toplis appeared before the Committee of Management of the Sun Fire Office and the chairman (William Shawe, the Sun's Treasurer – others present were the Secretary, Phillip Bewicke, Mr Ladbroke and Mr Littledale) communicated to him that he was 'appointed to the office of Surveyor of Stock to this Society'. Evidently they had confidence that he would prove to be a zealous and trustworthy servant: their confidence was not misplaced.

The appointment must have come as a relief to James Toplis, for he had not had a good year. In 1809–10 he had moved his business to 30 St Paul's Churchyard. In the eighteenth century it was usual for trades to congregate together in the same areas and the same streets, and St Paul's Churchyard was a centre for upholders. In 1800 there were no fewer than seven of them in a street of 36 shops: no. 4, Thomas Silk; no. 7, Graham & Son; no. 12, William Yateman; no. 18, George Beauchamp; no. 19, George Simon; no. 22, Oakley & Shackleton; and no. 26, William Morris. Some might think that there were enough upholders in one street, but it seems that the restaurant principle applied in those days: start a business where people know they will find good service in your trade.

James and his wife Mary settled into their new home with their two little boys James and Charles Hedges, who must have been about five and three years old respectively. Mary was seven months pregnant with her third child when disaster struck. On 1 May 1810

> at about half-past 11 o'clock, an alarming fire broke out at Mr Toplis's, upholsterer and cabinet-maker, in St Paul's Church-yard, which raged with great fury; but, fortunately, by the timely arrival of several engines, and a copious supply of water, its ravages were prevented extending beyond the premises where it began.

That was the account in *The Times*. Evidently there was such general relief that St Paul's Cathedral had not been burnt down yet again, that people tended to overlook the effect on poor James Toplis, his family and business. Indeed, another account says cheerfully that the fire was

> prevented from doing any other damage than totally destroying the whole of the premises where it first began.

'Any other damage'? James Toplis no doubt took a less sanguine view than the reporter from the *Gentleman's Magazine*. We must hope that James Toplis was fully insured. He must have been greatly relieved, six months later, to land the well-paid part-time job as Surveyor of Stock to the Sun Fire Office. At the same time he seems to have moved his own business rapidly down the street to no. 22,

5

the former premises of the upholders Oakley, Shackleton & Evans, where he advertised himself as 'Jas. Toplis, Upholsterer &c.' It was a handsome double-fronted house, and he proudly put his name over the door. Within two years he was prospering sufficiently to expand; as his sons were still children, he took a Mr John Woolfitt into the business as a partner, and in 1813, the firm became Toplis & Woolfitt. The partnership lasted until 1820 when Woolfitt started his own business at 3 St Paul's Churchyard, and the older firm became Toplis & Co.

On 14 July 1811, eight weeks after the fire, Mary Toplis gave birth to their third son, who was baptized that autumn in the parish of St Gregory by St Paul's, and given the names of Henry John Fuller. The parish of St Gregory was a curious anachronism, since no church existed at this time. The church had been at the south-west corner of the old St Paul's; it was named after Pope Gregory who had sent Augustine to convert England. Burnt down with the old cathedral in the Great Fire, it was not rebuilt, and the parish was united with its neighbour St Mary Magdalene, Knightrider Street.

Another familiar name appears in the registers of St Gregory's at this time: the son and daughter of Thomas and Elizabeth Harding were baptized in 1809 and 1812. Thomas Harding was a carpenter in Creed Lane, and it is scarcely credible that a carpenter (Harding) and a cabinet-maker (Toplis) would not have known each other. Unfortunately the Hardings seem to have moved out of the parish around 1815, and William Daniel Harding – who was subsequently to work for and later succeed James Toplis – must have been born *c.*1820. But it seems very likely that the families of Toplis and Harding knew each other in St Paul's Churchyard in the 1800s.

The Toplis family grew with a quartet of girls: Jane (b. 18 Oct. 1812), Ellen (b. 23 Dec. 1814), Fanny (b. 12 Nov. 1815) and Sarah Ellen (b. 3 Sept. 1818). There was then a gap, and it seems sadly that their mother Mary Toplis died. For it was another ten years before, on 12 Oct. 1829, a daughter was born to James and his second wife Ann Toplis: poignantly, they named her Mary, presumably after the first wife. There followed over the next few years a second family: another son, Edward, and two more daughters, Laura and Annie. By that time the family had moved its home out of the City, to the suburban setting of Southampton Place, Euston Square.

James Toplis therefore produced four sons and seven daughters; but it seems that of the sons only two, James Toplis and Charles Hedges Toplis, joined him in business. This by 1824 had developed from an upholsterers' into an auctioneering house, as a consequence of the association of the partners with the leading insurance companies. This is demonstrated by a handbill that survives from a sale by auction on 10 June 1824 by 'Mr Toplis' at a warehouse in Little Carter Lane of salvage recovered from a fire at King & Gregson's, Friday Street; the salvage consisted of

a quantity of Striped Muslins, Muslin Dresses, Berkley Handkerchiefs, about 100 pieces of Nainsooks [a cotton fabric from India, similar to muslin], 240 pieces of Loom, Books, and Jaconots [another cotton cloth], and a quantity of Work'd Trimmings and Flounces, Dyed Cambrics &c.

The sale was

By Order and on Account of the Directors of the Royal Exchange, Sun, and West of England Fire Offices.

Two years later, James Toplis jun. was admitted to the Freedom of the Upholders' Company 'by patrimony', and the business became Toplis & Son. Four years after that, in 1830, his younger brother Charles Hedges Toplis also joined the Livery. The presence of two sons in the business obviously liberated James Toplis sen. to take a more active

Auction Bill, 1824.

SALVAGE
Muslin, Muslin Dresses, Trimmings, &c.
WHICH WILL BE
Sold by Auction,
BY
MR. TOPLIS,

AT A WAREHOUSE,
In Little Carter Lane, St. Paul's,

On THURSDAY, June 10, 1824,
AT TWELVE O'CLOCK,

By Order and on Account of the Directors of the Royal Exchange, Sun, and West of England Fire Offices,

PART OF THE SALVAGE,
Saved from the late FIRE at Messrs. KING and GREGSON'S, FRIDAY STREET,

COMPRISING
A quantity of Striped Muslins, Muslin Dresses, Berkley Handkerchiefs, about 100 Pieces of Nainsooks, 240 Pieces of Loom, Books, and Jaconots, and a quantity of Work'd Trimmings and Flounces, Dyed Cambrics, &c.

Lot 1 About thirty pieces of green leno and a quantity of striped muslin
2 Thirty pieces of Berkley handkerchiefs
3 Thirty do
4 Forty do.
5 Seventeen pieces of 9-8ths pink cambric
6 Twenty-four coloured gingham dresses
7 Twenty do.
8 Twenty-two pieces 9-8ths coloured muslin
9 Ten do. 9-8ths blue cambric
10 Thirty-four do. coloured muslin dresses
11 Twenty-three do. nainsooks
12 About 16 do.   do.
13 About Seventeen do
14 About Sixteen do.
15 About Twenty-eight do.
16 Seventeen do, loom books and jaconots
17 Twenty-six do.
18 Twenty-four do.
19 About 30 do.   do.
20 Do.   do.
21 Do.   do.
22 Do.   do.
23 Do.   do.
24 Do.   do.
25 Sundry do. and striped muslin
26 A quantity of trimmings and flounces
27 Ditto
28 Ditto
29 Ditto
30 Ditto
31 Eleven pieces loom books, and 1 piece jaconot
32 Nine do.   do.   4 pieces lawn books, and 1 do. jaconot
33 Sundries
34 Ditto
35 Ditto
36 Ditto

May be Viewed on the Morning of SALE, and CATALOGUES had of Mr. TOPLIS, 22, St. Paul's Churchyard.

7

role in the Upholders' Company. In 1834 he was elected to the Court of Assistants, progressing through Junior Warden and Senior Warden until in 1836 he was elected Master, at the age of 50. But James Toplis was still working for the Sun Fire Office as surveyor, and travelling in their interest: in 1839 it is recorded that he made enquiries on their behalf in Limerick in Ireland, and in Mansfield in the East Midlands.

No doubt because of this long-established and continuing association with the Sun, James Toplis personally took charge of one of the most important auctions in 1841: on Monday 4 January, he disposed of the contents of St Bartholomew's church, across the road from the site of the Royal Exchange (which had been totally destroyed by fire three years earlier). As part of the rebuilding plans, it was agreed that a row of eighteenth-century houses standing between the Royal Exchange and the Mansion House would be demolished, to provide the triangular piazza that still exists. One of the occupiers of Bank Buildings, as the doomed row was called, was the Sun Fire Office, which therefore had to look for a new home.

The Bank of England was known to be seeking powers to demolish the church and other buildings on Threadneedle Street, and it seemed likely that a prime site would then become available on the corner of Bartholomew Lane, on which the Sun Fire Office could build a new head office appropriate to its growing importance. All this happened, and in due course James Toplis conducted the auction in St Bartholomew's church. As *The Times* reported on 5 January 1841:

> Yesterday the remains of the church, built after the fire of London, agreeably to Sir C. Wren's plans for rebuilding several churches and other public edifices, were brought to the hammer, Mr Toplis, the auctioneer, officiating on the occasion. It is being pulled down (in fact it is now a mere shell) to make way for the improvements attendant upon the rebuilding of the Royal Exchange . . .
>
> There only remained the flooring of the organ-loft and the forms on which the charity boys used to sit. The recess forming the vestry was the station selected by the auctioneer for his rostrum; and around him and over his head appeared chalked inscriptions intimating 'not for sale'. This recess, which in reality is part of the older building, is to remain; it is to be worked into the new house (a fire-office) to be erected at the corner of Bartholomew Lane. The building was investigated by vast numbers of persons during the day.

The need to raise money from this demolition was the more acute because at that time the Bishop of London and the freeholders of adjoining properties were making substantial claims for compensation. The wrangles were not resolved until March 1841, when the Sun was able to go forward and seek tenders for its new building; and indeed there was yet more trouble when the City required, a week before building started, that the building line should be moved back to provide wider streets. (The story is described in P. G. M. Dickson: *The Sun Insurance Office, 1710–1960.*)

Two years later, in 1843, it was James Toplis who represented the Sun in assessing the damage to the Marquis of Bute's house at Luton Hoo, which was virtually destroyed by fire on the night of 9 November. An under-gardener, sleeping in the basement, was woken at two o'clock in the morning by the sound of the fire, which had already gained a strong hold. He woke the housekeeper, Mrs Partridge, and they were joined by other staff and farm labourers in an attempt to save what they could. But by the morning the house was a smoking ruin, with only parts of the façade and the library remaining.

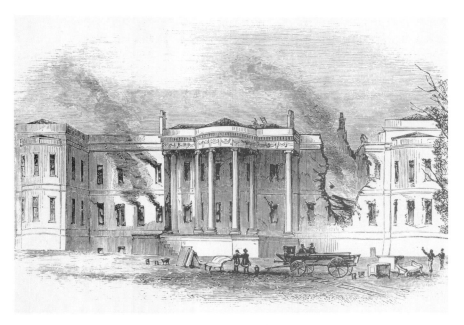

Luton Hoo after the fire, 1843.

The *Illustrated London News* noted that

> Mr Toplis, the Surveyor to the Sun Fire-office, has estimated the cost of restoring the building at between £30,000 and £40,000.

That was presumably an assessment on the building alone, rather than the contents: for another estimate of the damage suggested that it would far exceed the insurance. Useful and of some interest is the list of actual insurances thought appropriate to a great country house in the early years of Queen Victoria's reign:

> In the Sun fire-office the house and offices were insured for £10,000, the household goods for £10,000, the pictures and prints for £16,500, and the stables for £2,000; total £38,500. In the Phoenix-office, the household goods, for £10,000. In the Royal Exchange-office, the pictures and prints for £9,450. Gross total, £58,950.

It was fortunate that, largely due to the personal efforts of the housekeeper, a number of important paintings were saved, since she took a knife and cut them out of their frames – instructing her fellow-workers, while the fire dropped debris upon them, which of the pictures should have priority. The *Illustrated London News* even published an ode (a rather odd ode, perhaps) in her honour.

Complimentary Ode to Mrs Partridge

In spite
Of your fright
And the general flare
To take a case-knife
At the risk of your life
And cut out the paintings
(Without any faintings)
And fast in your gripe
Hold Raphael and Cuyp,
Caracci and Rubens, –
And very much *jubens*
(Latin's convenient sometime)
To save a fine Titian
What bangs every Grecian –
Zeuxis – Apelles,
Parhassius and fellows
Whose outlandish names will not rhyme!
A heroine
Most genuine
Are you, dear Mrs Partridge!

10

In the following year, 1844, James Toplis sen. took William Daniel Harding into the firm. Harding was then 24, a qualified surveyor. It seems very likely that the reason for this introduction was the illness or premature death of James Toplis jun. Probably he predeceased his father, for he is not mentioned in the latter's will (of 1861). The second son, Charles Hedges Toplis, also left the business at about this time, for in 1845 he is recorded as an artist, living at 6 Russell Place, Fitzroy Square.

Nevertheless, Toplis & Son of 16 St Paul's Churchyard remained a leader among London auction houses. The new address was a house on the corner of the narrow street known as Paul's Chain, and was thus a prime corner site. The scope of the activities of Toplis & Son is demonstrated by a sale held at Hexton House, Hertfordshire, on 15 February 1848 and the five following days. The catalogue, listing more than a thousand lots, describes the contents as 'the Furniture, Apollonicon Organ, two Piano Fortes, Farming Stock, Carriages and Horses, and Effects'. The furniture is described as 'recently supplied by and entirely from Messrs. Johnstone & Jeanes, of New Bond Street'.

Hexton House Sale Catalogue.

HEXTON HOUSE, HERTS.

Five-and-half miles from Hitchin.

A CATALOGUE

OF THE

𝕮𝖔𝖘𝖙𝖑𝖞 𝕱𝖚𝖗𝖓𝖎𝖙𝖚𝖗𝖊

OF THE ABOVE MANSION,

RECENTLY SUPPLIED BY AND ENTIRELY FROM

Messrs. JOHNSTONE & JEANES, of New Bond Street,

IT COMPRISES

SUPERIOR CHAMBER APPENDAGES,

IN MAHOGANY AND SATINWOOD,

Marble Washstands and Toilette Tables, Winged Wardrobes,

ROSEWOOD DRAWING-ROOM FURNITURE

In Chintz, with Curtains complete;

A SOLID CARVED OAK DINING - ROOM SUITE,

In Sideboard, Side Tables, Eighteen Chairs in Morocco,

Set of Expanding and Extending Dining Tables,

OR-MOLU CHANDELIERS AND LAMPS,

Self-acting Piano Forte by Rolfe, Horizontal Grand do. by Broadwood

APOLLONICON ORGAN,

VALUABLE PAINTINGS

BY ESTEEMED MASTERS,

THE FARMING STOCK

Including 11 Cows, 3 Calves, a Stirk, Hay, Wheat, Beans, Oats, Barley, &c.

CARRIAGES AND HORSES,

And a multitude of valuable items;

WHICH WILL BE SOLD BY AUCTION, BY

TOPLIS & SON

ON THE PREMISES,

On TUESDAY, FEBRUARY 15th, 1848, and Five following days,

AT TWELVE O'CLOCK PUNCTUALLY.

May be Viewed on Saturday and Monday preceding, and Mornings of Sale, by Catalogues only, (at One Shilling each) which may be had at the Library, Hertford; Post Office, Hitchin; on the Premises; and of TOPLIS and SON, 16, St. Paul's Church Yard, London.

Hexton must have been a most impressive home. In the entrance hall, for example, apart from the expected 'mahogany hat and umbrella stand' and 'a carved oak stem mounted with splendid antlers and massive oak base for hats and umbrellas' were two stuffed Bengal tigers, a stuffed African lioness, and two stuffed leopards. Clearly the family was musical, for the organ gallery was furnished with an Apollonicon organ. This was a popular instrument among wealthy Victorians with artistic tastes. Made by Benjamin Flight and Joseph Robson in London, it could be played by several performers, or mechanically, using barrels on which the tunes were picked out with pins (this one had 'six barrels arranged with the most favourite airs'; its case was decorated with a 'carved eagle and gilt pipes').

There were two other impressive musical instruments in the sale; in the dining room, a 'self-acting Grand Cabinet Piano Forte' by Rolfe (of London): this was another mechanical instrument, played by barrels. In the library, however, was a large grand piano in rosewood made by Broadwood (no doubt the model that Chopin played during his visit to Britain later that same year, 1848). But the family enjoyed other interests. There were some fine paintings: a Tintoretto, a Vandyke, eight Titians, a Ruysdael, and a Wilkie (though Mr Toplis noted in the catalogue that this was a clever copy). In the principal bedroom was a 'chance board' (for backgammon, perhaps) and a 'camera obscura'. In the library, together with ranks of Homer and Virgil, were copies of the *Racing Calendar, Hawker on Shooting*, Wait's *Army List*, and *Information to Travellers*.

More than a few pieces of furniture were French. In a bedroom was a 'blue and gilt japanned French bedstead with tester and backboard'; the library had 'French chintz curtains'. The sale was a strange mixture of the ostentatious and the commonplace. In the Grand Dining Room was 'a massive and highly enriched Or-molu Chandelier for 36 wax lights', and downstairs in the store were 178 pots of jam, 'various', and 'five jars of pickles'. In the stables, sold with the farm animals, were the family's horses and ponies: 'a Dun Pony, Taffy; a Grey Mare, Gwenellen; a Red Roan Saddle Mare, Winniford; a Brown Pony, Fag; and a Black Pony, Sheriff'. The last two are described as 'aged'.

What kind of a family would live in a house like this? Hexton is set in a curious peninsula of Hertfordshire, five miles north-west of Hitchin, that penetrates into Bedfordshire. The Hexton estate was bought in 1789 by William Young, a natural son of the fifth Baron Elibank (who commanded the marines in various battles). William Young died in 1824. His two daughters, Jane and Caroline were doubtless the musically inclined members of the family. Jane was accidentally drowned, and the Hexton estate devolved on her sister Caroline.

Caroline had married a French aristocrat, Joseph Andrew de Lautour, whose family were merchants and bankers in India (where he was born). Joseph Lautour's family came from Alsace, but sensibly went into exile shortly before the French Revolution. Joseph and Caroline certainly took their local responsibilities seriously, since in 1824 they rebuilt the parish church, and later endowed the village school. But their large financial resources became overstretched and in 1841 local creditors obtained court orders against Joseph for debt: one of them, Samuel Veazey of Baldock, took possession of the entire contents of Hexton, valued at over £6000, which he then leased back to the Lautours for £400 a year.

Joseph Lautour died in Paris in 1845, leaving Caroline at Hexton. She was evidently troubled by continuing debt, since it is said that bailiffs arrived to distrain upon household effects. Caroline invited them into the dining room where she plied them with excellent food and drink. When they had become 'a little fuddled', she made an excuse and left, locking the door behind her. She then went round and locked the other door, ordered her yellow carriage and her four best horses, hastily packed some clothes and her jewellery, and drove with all speed to the coast. She crossed over to France that evening. Later she took her daughters (and her yellow carriage) to Brussels, where she lived in considerable style.

Evidently in 1848 the creditors decided to foreclose, and put the contents of Hexton up for sale. Not everything went, since the 'elegant mahogany sideboard', from which Caroline fed the bailiffs, remains there to this day. Caroline returned to Hexton in later years, her finances evidently restored, playing her role as the respected Lady of the Manor until her death in 1869.

Her eldest son, William Francis Joseph de Lautour, was educated at Harrow and played cricket for England. He lived at Hexton (where he married, and produced six sons and four daughters). In 1870 he reverted (by deed poll) to his grandfather's surname, and became W. F. J. Young. (He died in 1899, and is buried outside the porch of Hexton Church.)

The copy of the catalogue that survives does not indicate the results of the sale. It may be assumed that as head of the firm, James Toplis conducted it himself, though no doubt he was assisted by W. D. Harding, who had now been working for him for almost four years. The catalogue is decorated with a pleasant little colophon or 'logo', an intertwined 'JT', indicating that James Toplis was well ahead of his time in the use of such identity marks. William Daniel Harding proved his usefulness, but it was not until a decade later, in 1857, that James Toplis rewarded him with a partnership and the firm became Toplis Son and Harding.

By this time James Toplis was 81 years old and no doubt felt he deserved retirement. He had earlier bought a house and farm at Boxted in Essex, some miles north of Colchester on the borders of Suffolk – fertile countryside, near the River Stour, 'Constable country'. He lived out his last years as a country gentleman, far from the bustle of Victorian London.

James Toplis sen. died at his home in Boxted on 8 November 1861. He was 85 years old and had been in good health; his doctor gave 'old age' as the cause of death, with 'congestion of the liver', which perhaps suggests that he liked the occasional glass. In his will he instructed that his funeral was to be 'without pomp or ostentation and with the greatest regard to economy'. His executors were two of his sons-in-law: Thomas Fox of Bishopsgate, upholsterer, and Henry Cheffins of Easton Manor in Essex. The estate was put in trust for his wife and daughters, his wife allowed to remain rent-free in the house but the farm to be sold. Old James made generous bequests – rather too generous, for they exceeded the value of his effects which was under £6000. No doubt he had made benevolent dispositions of his wealth in earlier years.

He could look back on a long and successful life, knowing that the business he had created in St Paul's Churchyard was thriving, high in reputation as one of the leading 'auctioneers, appraisers and surveyors' (as its partners now described themselves) in the City of London.

2. The Tooley Street Fire

BY 1861 William Daniel Harding was well established as senior partner of the firm which was at this time styled Toplis Son and Harding. Possibly, as shown earlier, he had known the Toplis family from boyhood. He was born in 1820; by 1861 he and his wife Caroline had three small sons – William Daniel jun., who was rising ten, Edward Ernest, who was eight, and the baby Harry Laurie, who was five. The Hardings had already moved house once in their married life, from their first home at 34 Murray Street in Hoxton New Town to a larger and more fashionable house at 4 Halliford Street, Islington.

William Daniel Harding.

16

The Toplis sons had now left the firm, though two of them survived for some years: Henry John Fuller Toplis died at the age of 61 in 1872, leaving his wife Lucy an estate of under £600; his brother, the artist Charles Hedges Toplis, lived nearly as long as his father, dying in Lambeth in 1886 at the age of 79. The name Toplis appears elsewhere in London in the 1860s. The firm originally called Toplis and Toplis, and from 1860 Toplis and Roberts, advertised itself in Conduit Street, Westminster, as 'auctioneers, surveyors and valuers and assessors to the Westminster Fire Office'. However, very little information has survived about this firm, and there is no recorded connection with the older firm in St Paul's Churchyard.

The history of the loss adjusting profession (*Order out of Chaos*: E. F. Cato Carter, Chartered Institute of Loss Adjusters, 1984) indicates that Roberts's firm was referred to in a court case in 1864 as 'fire loss adjusters', but that Roberts corrected the designation to 'auctioneer and valuer'. This seems to indicate that he, in common with his contemporaries, 'had yet to become a full-time independent fire loss adjuster at that time. The number of claims was insufficient to support the men seeking to build up an assessing practice.'

But the year 1861 was never to be forgotten in the world of London insurance. On Saturday 22 June in that year fire broke out in the warehouses of Tooley Street, Bermondsey, on the south side of the Thames opposite the Tower of London. The fire began in Cotton Wharf and, despite the efforts of the firemen of the private brigade led by James Braidwood and funded by the Fire Insurance offices, was soon out of control. It spread to Hays Wharf and Davis's Wharf, and the 'fearful conflagration' burned for four days and nights. The warehouses contained many types of goods and some – such as jute and hemp – were like dry tinder in the summer. Other wharves housed tallow tar and resin, which melted and poured into the river, so that at one point the Thames itself seemed to be on fire and several vessels, including an American steamship, were engulfed.

On the first evening of the fire Braidwood was killed when a warehouse containing saltpetre exploded. There were fears that, if the wind changed, the fire would spread into the congested houses of Bermondsey. In spite of that, great crowds gathered to see this extra-ordinary cataclysm, the worst of its kind in London since the Great Fire. The flames and smoke could be seen for fifty miles, and in spite of the danger, sightseers hired boats to gaze at the blazing buildings from the river. Although the fire above ground was controlled within a week, there was a constant danger for many days longer because hot molten tallow had flooded the underground vaults and, day after day, new fires broke out. On the twelfth day it was reported that

> a more threatening aspect is presented by the burning ruins than a
> week ago. The flames may be seen through several openings for an
> immense distance, like an underground lake of fire.

*The Tooley Street fire: a view from Cotton's Yard of the point where
Braidwood was killed.*

For six months smouldering embers could still be found on the site.
The commercial loss was immense. On the first Saturday the
Economist said:

> About 17,000 bales of Surat cotton, and 6,000 Tinnevelly, are entirely
> destroyed; while the large quantity of bacon, about 2,000 bales, either
> consumed or consuming in the burning ruins, has augmented the
> price, and placed dealers in a very awkward position, not a bale of fine
> bacon being left in the market. 300 tons of olive oil, 30,000 packages of
> tea, 900 tons of sugar, 427 cases of castor oil, and 8,800 casks of tallow,
> form but a few amongst many of the goods consumed, or now at the
> mercy of the devouring element.

The total value of property destroyed in the Tooley Street fire was eventually estimated at between £1 and £2 million. London merchants petitioned the Lord Mayor for assistance, because the fire 'was of an extent never equalled in the metropolis since the foundation of the Insurance Offices'. The Sun Office alone paid out £82,000 in losses. The value of the goods lost in the main Tooley Street fire had to be written off, since virtually nothing could be salvaged from that terrible conflagration.

Fires continued to break out along the south bank of the Thames. On 1 August 1861 a fire started in the warehouse of Messrs Curling & Co., known as Davis's Wharf, at Horselydown (it is approximately where the south end of the present Tower Bridge now emerges, though of course that bridge was not built until 25 years later). The fire began in the midst of a large warehouse, 300 ft by 100 ft and 40 ft high, filled with jute and Manilla hemp. By ten o'clock that morning the building was a blazing mass and the neighbouring premises were in imminent danger.

> Immediately opposite, within ten feet, is a range of buildings filled with saltpetre, the door and windows of which are scorched black [reported the *Illustrated London News*], and it required no small exertion on the part of the firemen to prevent these being consumed. At the east end of Messrs Curlings' shed . . . is another store filled with tallow, and adjoining that the well-known brewery of Messrs Courage & Co. Messengers were despatched to all the metropolitan engine-stations, and the engines, including the powerful steam-engine of Messrs Shand and Mason of Blackfriars-road, were soon on the spot. The steam-floats from Southwark-bridge and Rotherhithe were in requisition, and Mr Hodges, the distiller, also brought his engine, which was amongst the earliest at the scene. It is impossible to estimate the amount of damage done at present. Some thousands of tons of jute have been entirely or partially destroyed.

Naturally, someone had to estimate and appraise the loss and dispose of the salvage. Toplis Son and Harding had that job. W. D. Harding's financial account of the auction of salvage from the warehouse survives. It shows that in relation to Davis's Wharf, Horselydown, the Fire Offices paid out over £20,000. Harding's account describes the work done:

> To Proportion of expenses Working Salvage from Ruins, Van Hire, & Tolls, removing same to Field at Rotherhithe, and to Tan Yard at Bermondsey, Men and Women sorting same and putting in Lots for Sale, Rent of Depots, Watching Police expenses, Superintendence,

Compensation to Mr Ledger, for damage to his Garden, Commission on Sale, preparing and printing Accounts, &c., £17.17 per Cent.

He held three auctions, on 30 August, 12 and 13 September and 19 September, at which he sold the salvaged jute and hemp for £8,590 7d, less his firm's fees of £1,535 8s. 6d. This is a very large fee indeed but it is clear that through Harding's exertions in relation to this wharf, the Fire Offices recovered rather more than a third of their losses in this unprecedented disaster. It involved a great deal of work over a long period: he was still sending out cheques in December. The account also shows that most of the leading insurance offices were involved, including the Sun, Phoenix, and Royal Exchange.

Tooley Street remained a matter of public concern and indeed the danger of renewed fires lingered on until the smouldering embers were finally extinguished by torrential rainstorms during October and November. National interest in the devastation was overtaken, however, in December 1861 by the death of Prince Albert, the Prince Consort.

The losses sustained by the insurers in the Tooley Street fire and its aftermath were unprecedented and considerable and they demanded that fire protection should become a national responsibility. It was directly as a consequence of the Tooley Street conflagration that on 1 January 1866 the Government established the Metropolitan Fire Brigade in London.

The creation of a fire brigade for the metropolis did not, unfortunately, prevent fires from breaking out from time to time. In 1866 W. D. Harding auctioned the salvage from two other London fires, both involved with jute or hemp: on 16 March, Messrs Watson Metcalf's warehouse in Burr Street, East Smithfield, went up in flames with a loss of £17,520 worth of hemp; and a month later, on 27 April, the North Quay warehouse at the East India Docks was burned down with a loss of £9,510 worth of jute.

Not all the sales were on that scale. In November 1867 Toplis and Harding (as the firm was now styled) advertised a sale at their rooms, now at 16 St Paul's Churchyard, 'At One Punctually, on Account of the Fire Insurance Companies', of

the Salvage Stock of a Wholesale Boot and Shoe Manufacturer, Hosier and Draper –
4,000 pairs Boots and Shoes, Coats, Trousers & Vests, Melton, Doe, Cashmere, Calf and Morocco Skins and Uppers, Buttons, Webbing &c. & General Drapery.

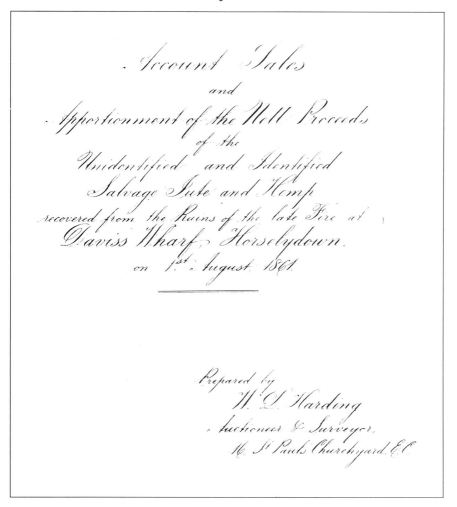

Account Sales

and

Apportionment of the Nett Proceeds

of the

Unidentified and Identified

Salvage Jute and Hemp

recovered from the Ruins of the late Fire at

Daviss Wharf, Horselydown.

on 1st August 1861

Prepared by

W. D. Harding

Auctioneer & Surveyor,

16 St Pauls Churchyard. E.C.

Cover of W. D. Harding's accounts following the Tooley Street fire.

Now the firm described its activities as those of 'Auctioneers, Surveyors & Estate Agents'. But this was very much in association with the major insurance companies, and particularly with the Fire Offices. A decade later Toplis and Harding was one of the firms in competition for the business of the Alliance office. The firm was therefore recognized as being among the leaders in this work.

3. The Pantechnicon

IT WAS in the 1860s that the professionalism of the fire assessor came to be tested. Since insurance on land (as distinct from marine risks) was largely concerned with fire risks, the increasing competition between the insurance companies led to public suspicion that they were extending themselves into areas of extreme risk and then paying out on doubtful claims in order to undercut their competitors. Earlier in the century there had been informal contacts between the three major companies then in existence, the *Sun* (for which James Toplis acted as assessor), the *Phoenix* and the *Royal Exchange*. But by the 1860s these links had been much strained by the pressure of new competition. Even so, they co-operated in matters that were regarded as of common interest in the Fire Offices' Committee.

Public unease led to the setting up in 1867 of a Select Parliamentary Committee on Fire Protection, which took evidence from a number of insurance companies and from the Metropolitan Fire Brigade. The latter was represented by Captain Eyre Massey Shaw (later to be regarded as one of the great figures in London fire fighting, but at this time still comparatively new in his job and feeling his way). Captain Shaw agreed that in 1866 the proportion of unknown causes of fires in London was 44 per cent and agreed that the number of suspicious fires seemed to be increasing.

One of the points made by the Select Committee in its report was that

> It has further been given in evidence, and admitted even by gentlemen connected with insurance companies, that the increase in the number of fires in late years is in some measure to be attributed to the great competition among insurance companies for business; to their carelessness in taking risks, as well as in their appointment of agents; to the too ready facility with which they settle claims, some of which they believe to be fraudulent; and to a disinclination in general in the companies to prosecute. The reasons given for this disinclination . . . are, the great difficulty of obtaining evidence, the want of proper means of compelling them to do so, the prejudice existing in the public

mind and in the minds of juries against public companies prosecuting private individuals, the unpopularity to which a prosecution exposes them, and the uncertainty of the result.

This led to the Select Committee's recommendation that an inquiry should take place into every fire, in three stages: the first should be made by the Police or Fire Brigade, and if they were suspicious of the causes of the fire, they should report the matter to the Coroner (in England) who would be empowered to examine witnesses on oath, possibly before a jury; and if a case seemed to be made out, the accused would be prosecuted in the criminal courts.

These proceedings are described in great detail in E. F. Cato Carter's history of the loss adjusting profession, *Order Out of Chaos*, published in 1984 by the Chartered Institute of Loss Adjusters. It is clear that one consequence of the report of the Select Committee on Fire Protection was that it encouraged the fire insurance companies to arrange for much more accurate and precise investigations to be made into fires before easily accepting claims. It is reported that there was a considerable increase in the number of claims found to be fraudulent in court proceedings, including four instances of the arrest and prosecution of arsonists. Among the assessors, whose reports led to these proceedings, was W. D. Harding of Toplis and Harding.

Steps towards the formalization of the assessor's role then inevitably followed, since it was quite usual for the insured to hold policies with two or more companies. One of the functions of an assessor was to apportion the proportion of any loss between the various companies. It was necessary, therefore, for there to be complete confidence between the assessors and the insurers. For their part, the Fire Offices' Committee set about preparing a 'List of Valuers to be employed in the settlement of losses in which two or more offices are concerned which may occur in the Southern District' (the Southern District encompassed most of England from Manchester southwards). The list was approved at a meeting of the Fire Offices' Committee on 1 May 1873 and distributed to the 43 representatives present. Among the 46 'Valuers' (or assessors) on that list were Messrs. Toplis and Harding of 16 St Paul's Churchyard. Their speciality (as between buildings and contents) was given as the contents of buildings affected by fire.

Only a few months later there was a major test of the efficiency of these arrangements. At about half past four on the afternoon of Friday 13 February 1874 the staff of the Pantechnicon warehouse in Belgravia smelt burning and discovered that there was a fire on the second floor. The Pantechnicon was a huge building (for the time), covering nearly two acres and stretching from Motcombe Street in the south to Lowndes Square in the north. It was full of costly goods, since the fashionable people in this wealthiest sector of Victorian London used customarily to shut up their town houses during the winter and hibernate in their country estates. As part of this procedure they would send their best furniture, silver and works of art to be stored at the Pantechnicon. The building was also used by the major London banks for the storage of deeds and plate deposited by their customers.

It had been built in 1830 by Seth Smith, whose grandson was one of the proprietors (Smith and Radermacher) at the time of the fire. The building was considered to be fireproof, since the main structure was iron, including pillars and floors, with stone stairs and a 'fireproof' roof; there was no exposed wood in the building. Furthermore, a strong sales pitch was made of the water tank 'of great size' on the roof.

When the fire began, therefore, the foremen and about 20 or 30 workmen tried to quell it. But it burnt furiously. Though there was indeed a large water tank on the roof, there were no hydrants in the building; and the manual fire engine quickly brought into use could not make any impression. The nearby iron fire doors were therefore closed and heavy tarpaulins spread on the goods in the floor below.

The Belgravia Pantechnicon.

24

The Pantechnicon fire.

The Metropolitan Fire Brigade (led by Captain Shaw) arrived with several steam and manual fire engines within 15 minutes and set to work. Troops were also drafted in from Knightsbridge, Chelsea and Wellington Barracks: Coldstream Guards, Scots Fusiliers and Life Guards. There was a livery stable nearby and the soldiers helped to lead out 150 horses who escaped safely. But the fire had caught a fierce hold and the Pantechnicon's 'fireproof' character proved to be illusory. Evidently the Fire Brigade found the same shortage of water that had defeated the local workmen. The fire raged through the evening and, shortly after ten o'clock, a large part of the roof of the south building suddenly fell in. The reflection of the flames could be seen as far away as Twickenham.

By the middle of the night the fire was beginning to die down, but the Fire Brigade was kept on the site through the following Saturday and Sunday. It was not for some days that the reckoning of the disaster could be made. The ruins became a new tourist attraction and those who had stored goods in the Pantechnicon found, when they went to look for their property, that they were hampered by unthinking sightseers. The place became such a talking-point that

25

even Queen Victoria visited it: two weeks after the fire her carriage stopped outside in Motcombe Street, the doors of the façade were thrown open, and the monarch gazed into the scene of devastation. Graciously she accepted an old and rare edition of Shakespeare, belonging to Major-General Benson CB, which had been recovered from the ruins virtually undamaged: the Queen added it to her collection of curios at Windsor. Or so one account has it; another report says that the Queen accepted an ivory elephant 'much blackened and discoloured' from Gen. Benson, and a jewelled dagger, a relic of the Indian Mutiny.

But then the insurance companies and their assessors had to begin

The fire seen from the roof of Rives' stables.

their work. Some customers had been fortunate. A few days before the fire, the Marquess of Westminster (he was created Duke later that year) removed a quantity of furniture and valuables to Eaton Hall. By chance, and coincidence, most of the bank deposits had also been taken away. Among the losers were many members of the Houses of Parliament; had the fire happened three weeks later, they would all have been back in town, and have safely reclaimed their goods, for Parliament was due to reassemble.

The building itself had cost £200,000 but was only insured for £20,000 (with the Royal Exchange). The proprietors also had to point out that they knew 'little or nothing of the actual contents of the private strong rooms or of their value'. On the insurance of articles deposited with them, they claimed to be 'only responsible for safe custody, and that the insurance must be made apart from them'. They agreed, however, that the customers had such faith in the building's reputation for being fireproof that many of them had felt it unnecessary to insure against fire. It was also admitted that to save the higher charges levied on the storage of (silver) plate, depositors were known to have put jewels, silver and other valuables in crates labelled as containing ordinary furniture.

A few days after the fire the Sun office was facing claims for upwards of £60,000, and the Law Fire Office of £18,650, of which 14,000 represented the insured value of a collection of pictures belonging to Sir Frederic Sykes (including four important paintings by Gainsborough). Soon afterwards the depositors' claims had risen to £130,000, but the fire companies estimated the total losses at around £3 millions. There were 21 fire offices involved. The first trawl of the ruins was done by assessor representatives of the Sun and Imperial offices, as probably bearing the largest liability (it was found that the plate room was virtually undamaged, but this was one of the few parts of the building that was). Then, once an agreement had been signed between the proprietors, the insurance companies and the depositors concerning payment for the search, the laborious process was begun by 40 men from the London Salvage Corps, who carted the recoverable items to a plot of land at South Kensington, and valuables to a hired schoolroom in Eccleston Street, where depositors could claim them.

A month after the conflagration it had to be admitted that very little had been saved. As *The Times* remarked on 16 March,

> It is now but too clear that the original expectation that a large and valuable salvage would be recovered will, unfortunately, not be realised. Almost everything seems to have been burnt to a cinder.

One of the most substantial losers was Sir Richard Wallace. A leading Victorian connoisseur, he inherited in 1870 the art collection of the Marquesses of Hertford (he was believed to be the natural son of one of them; his mother was Maria, Lady Hertford). Some at least of that great collection – regarded at the time as one of the finest in the world – perished in the Pantechnicon. He valued his deposits at £150,000 though they were insured for only a fraction of this. His collection of armour was recovered 'nearly complete, but very much burnt and broken'. With a collection of enamel dishes, these were insured with the Sun office for £30,000; and they were in

> as good a state of preservation, comparatively speaking, as anything that has yet come from the ruins, but they were damaged so much that the owner has declined to claim them, and has been paid by the companies the full amount of his insurance.

Enough remained elsewhere of the great collection for Sir Richard Wallace to bequeath it to the nation, on his death in 1890, to found the Wallace Collection in the Hertfords' London house.

Among other substantial losers were Wynne Ellis, who had built up the largest silk business in London as a haberdasher, hosier and mercer on Ludgate Hill, and made a second fortune buying property in the City. He bought many fine pictures, including more Gainsboroughs, and some at least were burnt up in the Pantechnicon. Ellis was in his 80th year, and died shortly after the fire, leaving his collection to the National Gallery, which rather churlishly only accepted 44 of them.

Several large libraries perished in the fire, and one Egyptian mummy. The basement was equipped for the storage of 3000 pipes of wine, whose loss must have depressed many. But probably the most regretted loss, in public opinion, was the furniture and household effects of General Sir Garnet Wolseley (afterwards Field Marshal Viscount Wolseley). Sir Garnet had shut up his house at Richmond and stored its contents in the Pantechnicon, on leaving England to command the British troops in the Ashanti Wars in West Africa. A popular figure, his personal standards were such that 'All Sir Garnet' was the Victorian synonym for 'all correct'. He had made his reputation during the Indian Mutiny, when his bravery had made him a Lieut. Colonel at 25, and he had been mentioned in despatches five times. Now, while fighting yet more battles of the British Empire, he lost many treasured possessions, including souvenirs of his campaigns in the Crimea, India, China and North America.

The Pantechnicon fire is therefore a particularly interesting reflection of the changing nature of fire insurance, and the growing awareness of the need for precision in the description of contents and of damage. It is also, incidentally, a fascinating guide to society in Britain in the high peak of prosperity in the Victorian age. Here are the Parliamentarians, not meeting during the winter; the county folk, closing their London houses to retire to the country; the distinguished soldiers, consolidating the British Empire.

What was the cause of this damaging fire? It was never precisely established, since the initiating fire was so fierce that little forensic evidence remained. The general belief was that a recent depositor had left a bottle of some flammable liquid (described as 'benzoline') inside a crate of kitchen equipment, and that the crate had been put directly against a hot flue. The crate was packed with straw, which of course fuelled the blaze.

Less than two months after the fire, a depositor who had lost everything wrote to *The Times* in fury, using the pseudonym 'A Sufferer'. He had just received an invoice from the management of the Pantechnicon: it was a rent bill for the past three months for furniture placed in the Pantechnicon for safe keeping. . . . (An unusually skittish sub-editor on the normally solemn *Times* headlined this: BURNING THE CANDLE AT BOTH ENDS.) On the following day another of the 2000 depositors capped this: the Pantechnicon management had added to the bill a hope that they might enjoy the depositors' further patronage. . . .

The Pantechnicon managers spoke up for themselves. They, too, they pointed out, had suffered loss. Other depositors wrote to support them; those who had not taken the trouble or expense to insure their property could not reasonably blame the warehouse managers for their loss. In the following autumn the rebuilding of the Pantechnicon began. So, no doubt, did the reconsideration of insurance cover in many Belgravia households.

William Daniel Harding sen. died at his home, 45 Lee Terrace, Lewisham, on 14 January 1885, at the age of 65. He left estate valued at £9765 11s. 5d., with bequests to his widow and sons. He left the goodwill of the business to his two sons William Daniel Harding jun. and Edward Ernest Harding in equal shares. He made a personal bequest to his friend and Lewisham neighbour Edward Charles Davies (who was co-executor with Harding's son Edward Ernest) of 'any one literary work out of my library which he may choose to select and I hope he will choose a good one and keep it in remembrance of me'.

In his will, W. D. Harding sen. wrote, 'William Hill Fiddaman has for many years been associated with me in my business and I have great respect for his business habits and I suggest (without creating any direction or trust) to my said sons William Daniel Harding and Edward Ernest Harding whether it would not be to their interest and advantage to admit the said William Hill Fiddaman in to partnership with them.' Harding also left Fiddaman a personal legacy of £500. There is no evidence that the sons took their father's advice in this matter. William Daniel Harding jun., the elder son, is believed to have joined the firm about 1870 (when he would have been 19) and to have left around 1880. His subsequent career is unknown. So the younger son, Edward Ernest Harding, became the senior partner in Toplis and Harding. He had already married and secured his succession: for his son Graham was born on 7 January 1879 at 19 Thomsett Road, Penge.

Sifting through the debris after the fire.

4. Into a New Century

IN 1890 the firm moved its offices to larger premises at 80 St Paul's Churchyard. Five years later, E. E. Harding took his 16-year-old son Graham into the firm as a pupil; and in the following year there was yet another office move, to 66 Cannon Street. In due course young Graham completed his apprenticeship and his father took him into partnership.

The business was changing. In 1907, Cato Carter records, one insurer mentioned 'the phenomenal rush to enter the field of accident insurance which has been witnessed during the past twelve months'. No doubt it was Graham Harding's youthful enthusiasm that led him to take the family firm into this new business; indeed, if there had been any slowing down in the development of Toplis and Harding in the last years of the nineteenth century, it was soon back among the leaders. Indeed, by 1911 it was one of the 'big firms' in the business, according to Roland Redfern, then a young assessor with Brown, Roberts, Radmall and Company (after the war he joined Toplis and Harding).

In 1907 Graham Harding married Dorothy Hollender. He was 28, and she was ten years younger. They married at the Theistic Church, St James's; theism – the belief in a God, or 'natural religion', based on the philosophies of Kant and Hegel – had attracted support in Edwardian England. The Hollender family had a connection with St James's, since the art gallery on the corner of St James's Street and Jermyn Street was run by 'Hollender & Koekkoek'. Dorothy gave her father's name as 'Max Hollender, deceased' and his rank or profession is shown on the marriage certificate as 'Count'. She had a strongly romantic streak which soon emerged in a series of popular novels written under the pseudonym 'Dolores Harding': the first of them was published in 1911.

Graham Harding's father Edward Ernest was not in good health. When he died, in Hastings in July 1910, he was only 56. He left £719 11s. 9d. Therefore Graham Harding became senior partner at the age of 30. Hitherto the firm had been operating almost entirely

31

for the Tariff Offices; but it was not long before a Lloyd's underwriter, Hubert Nicholls, sent for him on the recommendation of an official of the Alliance Assurance Company and asked him to take over the assessment of a particularly unpleasant and suspicious fire in the East End of London. This he did so competently that his work was noticed by Cuthbert Heath, a leading Lloyd's underwriter.

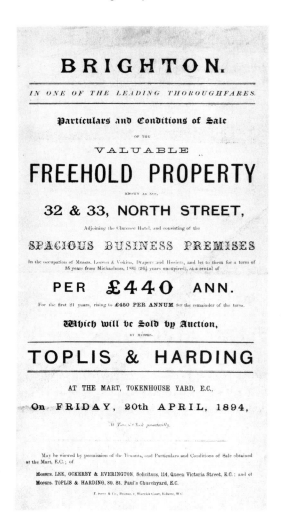

Sales Bill of an auction in Brighton by Toplis and Harding, 1844.

Cuthbert Heath was at this time one of the great innovators at Lloyd's. He had been working there for forty years, starting as an 18-year-old junior filling inkwells in the offices of Henry Head & Co. His ambition had been to go into the navy – his father was Admiral Sir Leopold Heath, beachmaster at the Crimea landings – but he suffered from chronic deafness. Becoming an underwriting member of Lloyd's at 21, he was soon making a name for himself. He began to write non-marine risks, and introduced loss-of-profits insurance. In the late 1880s there was a spate of burglaries in London (many carried out by the notorious Charles Peace and his emulators). A broker approached Cuthbert Heath to write fire insurance, and half-jokingly asked: 'You wouldn't add burglary, I suppose?' After a moment's thought, Heath answered: 'Why not?'

He was soon highly successful, and in 1890 formed his own broking partnership of C. E. Heath & Co. to provide his Lloyd's syndicate with still more business. But the main element in Heath's success was that he invariably based his assessment of risk, and thus his premiums, on the most detailed research. Before he began to underwrite earthquake and hurricane insurance, he prepared an 'earthquake book' which was compiled from all the old maps and literature that he could assemble. Whereas many of his predecessors at Lloyd's had based their business on rule-of-thumb, commonsense and indeed intelligent guesswork, Cuthbert Heath based his on proven historical and scientific evidence. He also widened his commercial activities, and in 1894 (rather with the disapproval of the Committee of Lloyd's) started his own insurance company, the Excess.

In April 1906 the San Francisco earthquake devastated that city. The total underwriting loss was £45 million, of which the British market carried one-quarter. Many American lawyers descended on London determined to find all the loopholes by which their insurance clients could avoid payment. But Cuthbert Heath cabled his San Francisco agent: 'Pay all our policy-holders in full irrespective of the terms of their policies.' The gesture made the reputation of Heath, and of Lloyd's of London, in the United States. Seven years earlier, a Lloyd's broker touring America had found enough business in a few months to bring him a commission of £1000 a year (then a huge sum). The United States had become the most important market for British fire insurance, which by 1900 accounted for at least 40 per cent of total premium income. By 1905 (records Barry Supple in his history of the Royal Exchange Assurance), the nine leading British companies – which between them accounted for about two-thirds of all fire premiums – earned half their £15.6 million premium income in the United States. Insurance business was booming in the USA, and among the most successful houses (founded in 1897) was Rollins Burdick Hunter of Chicago.

A year after the San Francisco earthquake, Rollins Burdick Hunter arranged the insurance in London of a steam motor car built by the White Sewing Machine Company. It was Lloyd's first American motor policy, and it was written by the Heath syndicate. In the following year, the head of the Chicago brokers, Charles Rollins, came to London to place some high-risk insurance for the vast meat stockyards of Chicago which covered many acres. The risk was high because the immense stockyards were almost entirely built of wood – floors, staircases, partitions. The fire risk was increased because meat-packers used wooden boxes to pack the meat; the scale of business was such that they had their own sawmills, in which the fire risk was even more considerable: the premium rates could be 12 per cent.

The business was written by C. E. Heath. It was a very big deal, and began a close association with the Chicago brokers: Rollins Burdick Hunter thereafter sent considerable amounts of business to Lloyd's of London, most to be written by Heath. This eventually included (in 1912) the writing of one of the first fleets of American trucks, and the first motor fleet for one of the meat-packing companies. There was another large piece of business, known as the 'branch-house floater', to provide cover of up to one-quarter of a million dollars on any one loss in the 700 branch-houses to which the packers sent their meat for distribution to butchers. When Swifts, one of the largest meat processors, started its own insurance company in 1907, its reinsurances were at first placed in the American market: but then Rollins Burdick Hunter began to place them with Heath in London. When, for tax reasons, the in-house insurance company, the Interstate Insurance Exchange, had to be wound up in 1912, the business was taken over by the Chicago brokers, and the reinsurances were written at Lloyd's under Heath's leadership.

One of the most remarkable of the Chicago deals was the initiation by Cuthbert Heath of a 'fire divisions' scheme of insurance. Rollins Burdick Hunter had planned a scheme which divided the huge areas of the Chicago meat stockyards into 27 divisions, each of which could be closed off with fire doors, to limit the spread of fire. Heath provided cover with a limit of $250,000 for each fire area. The policy would be honoured on the word of the company's fire risks manager who would confirm how many divisions had been affected by fire. This was the most extraordinarily liberal agreement since it relied entirely on the word of the assured.

It demonstrated the close bonds of trust developed at this time between the insurance leaders of Chicago and London. That Cuthbert Heath was by now a leader at Lloyd's is demonstrated by his part in the establishment in 1910 of the Lloyd's Non-Marine Underwriters' Association, the NMA. The essence of his business was that he would be personally in London, either in the office of C. E. Heath & Co. or in the Heath box at Lloyd's (after 1911, when the committee of Lloyd's objected to his use of his Excess Insurance Company literature in the Room, he went there less and less). Yet he had to be in London, but also needed to be personally represented from time to time in Chicago in the matter of claims. His representative had to be intelligent, knowledgeable about the business, hardheaded to deal with the tough go-getting world of expanding Chicago, but with the sort of easy cheerful manner that would appeal to the Americans. Graham Harding was tailor-made for the job.

5. Travelling Abroad

GRAHAM HARDING eagerly grasped the opportunity that his association with Heath gave him. He soon became an inveterate traveller. He made several journeys to the United States on behalf of Lloyd's, at Heath's invitation. He made friends and business contacts wherever he went, and it seemed to him that to have representatives in many parts of the world would enlarge his own business, not least because of the improvement and acceleration of modern communications through the telegraph and telephone. In 1911 he opened a North of England office, in Manchester (which had become familiar to him because the great Cunard liners on which he began his American journeys sailed from Liverpool; and that city and Manchester together formed the second most prosperous commercial centre in the country). He also opened an office in Paris, and often visited it on his way to and from foreign assignments.

His personal diary for 1914 gives a vivid indication of the sheer mileage he covered, which would tax many modern jet-setters (and Graham Harding's journeys, of course, were done entirely by train and ship). On 9 January 1914 he left Victoria station for Italy. On the following morning he called into the Paris office, then left for Trieste. Five days later he was back in Paris, and on the next day in London. Two weeks after that he set off for Tunisia, allowing himself two days in the Paris office before entraining for Marseilles and the sea journey across the Mediterranean. He spent two weeks in Tunisia, visiting Tunis, Bizerta, Kairouan and Sousse (this may have been a winter holiday in the sun). On his way back he spent a day in Nice, and a further day in the Paris office.

This time he was in England for six weeks. But on 17 April he was travelling in Europe again – to Lille, Paris, Berlin, Stockholm, St Petersburg (now Leningrad) and Archangel. He was in Archangel for a week, and then set off for home; it took him five days of train travel. (Evidently he made good friends at Archangel, for a 'panorama-postcard' exists with messages from his convivial companions: 'We clink our glasses to the absent noble foreigner', and –

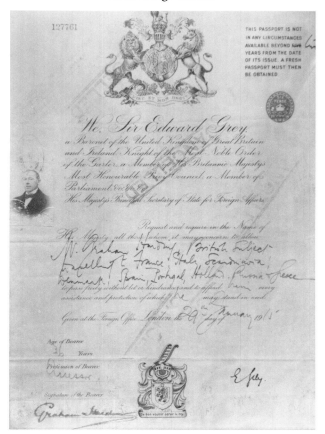

Graham Harding's passport, 1915.

more cryptically — 'The ice was go off, the business is finished, your health we drink in champagne, and wish you all goods of the world.')

Three weeks later he went over to the Paris office for three days. In mid-July he crossed the North Sea from Hull to Kristiansand in Norway; while there he visited a sanatorium at Flekkero. On July 31 his diary states, succinctly, 'War'. He anticipated slightly, for war with Germany was in fact declared by Great Britain on 4 August. This did not immediately affect the business, or even the Paris office: Graham Harding was there again at the beginning of November, on a journey (via Bordeaux and San Sebastian) to Portugal, where he visited Lisbon and the old capital, Evora. But soon the pressures of war meant that the Paris office had to be run down for the duration.

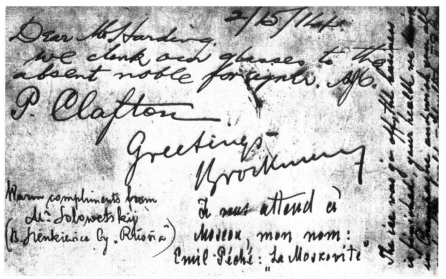

Message on postcard from Archangel to G. Harding, 1914.

During the war, Graham Harding served with the Royal Naval Reserve (though not very dramatically: at one point he was a telephonist stationed high on Tower Bridge to look for marauding Zeppelins. He was very deaf, and lost that job when he failed to answer an inspecting Admiral, who discovered his disability and had him moved to less exposed work). He also took a number of commissions from the Government for the assessment of war damage, particularly after the bombardment of the north-east coast of England by German battleships early on the morning of 16 December 1914, when people were killed or injured at West Hartlepool and there was considerable

The panorama-postcard.

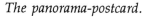

property damage there and at Scarborough. In this, Harding worked with a London solicitor, William Charles Crocker, specializing in insurance work and particularly associated with Lloyd's. Crocker (who became a close friend and associate of Graham Harding, and was to be his executor and trustee) gave an account of this episode in his autobiography *Far from Humdrum* (Hutchinson, London, 1967):

> In this hit-and-run raid nearly 500 civilians were killed or wounded. The great shells caused heavy damage to small houses. The Cabinet thought it politically expedient that those who had suffered in the attack should be compensated. My good friends Messrs. Toplis & Harding were instructed as government assessors for this purpose. The adjustment of claims for material loss was straightforward and proceeded on ordinary fire-insurance lines. The claims in respect of death and personal injuries presented a problem. By what standard were they to be measured? I vividly recall the thrill with which I received an invitation to help find an answer to that question. A modified version of my well-tried employers' liability 'Sausage Machine' worked at full speed and collected the facts upon which, whatever yardstick might be employed, compensation in each case must depend. It was a grand experience to meet the tough Yorkshire 'tykes' who were wholly unmoved by the 'frightfulness' which was meant to cow them. Their talks with me were terse and often grim. An old lady telling of her husband's end said, 'They scraped 'im off t' wall!'
>
> I set out several alternative scales from which the government might choose to measure the proposed awards. Among them was one (it happened to be the cheapest) which the minister-in-charge, Mr David Lloyd-George, saw fit to adopt. This assumed that the claims arose from injuries to workpeople and were adjustable under the provisions of the Workmen's Compensation Act. . . . All my figures had been carefully adjusted so that no one recipient could fairly say that he or she had been less favoured than another. What annoyed me was that the Cabinet quadrupled the compensation I had recommended

for one Mistress Marjorie Makepeace, a cockle-gatherer, and for no better reason than that her name and occupation were 'so delightfully Shakespearean'! This threw a monkey wrench into my nicely balanced machinery and doubtless led to the sort of jealous comparisons I had been at such pains to avoid.

Later in the war Toplis and Harding were among the many loss adjusters called in to assist with the aftermath of a terrible disaster, the Silvertown explosion in east London. On the evening of Friday 19 January 1917, fire broke out in the Brunner Mond Chemical Works, manufacturing TNT and nitro-glycerine. The chief chemist, Dr Andrea Angel, while ordering the evacuation of the building, personally led the desperate attempts to control the fire, fully aware of the almost inevitable consequences. The fire spread, and there was an explosion which left a crater 300 feet wide, lit up the whole of London, and was heard as far as Slough, 25 miles away. The explosion engulfed a fire engine, and two firemen were among the 46 bodies recovered from the debris.

The factory was surrounded by streets of small East End houses. Three whole streets of 600 houses were destroyed, and 1000 local people rendered homeless. The damage was horrendous. But insurance did not cover much of it. The managers of fire insurance companies were quoted (in *The Times*) as

> perfectly satisfied that the liability for, at any rate, the bulk of the damage is not theirs. Most ordinary fire policies contain a clause ruling out damage by explosion 'except explosion of boilers used for domestic purposes, or of the illuminating gas happening elsewhere than on premises in which gas is manufactured or stored'.

The bulk of the damage, they pointed out, had been caused not by fire but by an explosion. Windows had been broken over a wide area, but this damage would not be covered by most domestic policies. The exception might be plate-glass shop windows, which were often specifically insured against breakage.

The huge number of claims were co-ordinated by F. E. Eiloart, who as well as being a leading assessor was a Fellow of the Surveyors' Institution. He brought in many of his professional colleagues, Graham Harding among them, to help with the huge task. The immense job of repair and rebuilding was put in hand immediately, and within two months 804 houses had been re-roofed, slated and rendered waterproof; of those, 106 had been handed back to their occupiers. Also '44 shops, 395 houses, 8 stables and 1 church' had been handed over, the necessary repairs being completed.

Early in June, the House of Commons was told that

> The Ministry had instructed assessors to assess damage . . . for which claims have been made, and their recommendations are examined by the Ministry. It is only in very exceptional circumstances that after an assessor has made a recommendation it has been found necessary to make special inquiries, thus causing delay. Over 11,000 claims have been lodged. Of this number 5650 have been approved and 5585 actually paid. Nearly all the claims for personal injury and furniture have been met.

But it was a further three months before the Minister of Munitions, 'without admitting or assuming legal liability', told the House of Commons that he would

> consider favourably the payment (out of funds to which the manufacturers will contribute) of reasonable claims for compensation for personal injury or for loss arising from damage to property, directly attributable to the explosion (damage to the factory or injury to persons inside excluded).

It was a considerable tribute to the assessors that in such circumstances their judgement was both accepted and acted upon by the Government. Very large sums were involved: the overall cost of the Silvertown explosion and its aftermath was estimated at between £2 million and £2.5 million.

Harding's marriage did not survive the war. Though a daughter (Maxine) had been born to them, for some years he and his wife lived increasingly separate lives, as she continued her dedication to authorship. By 1918, when their marriage broke up, she had published three novels (*The Great Experiment, Affairs of Men,* and *Oranges and Lemons*: she was to publish a dozen novels, and edit two works of Spanish literature). Harding travelled extensively on business and pleasure, and in London was a gregarious clubman, as an active member of the Junior Carlton and the Royal Automobile Club. It was at the RAC that he met and fell in love with a lively and cheerful young Irishwoman, Winefride Anne Patricia Reardon (known as Pat). They married in London in the autumn of 1919, and went on honeymoon to Egypt, returning to his home at Erleigh Court, near Reading. In the thirties they moved to Woodcote End, Epsom. Two sons, Patrick and Wyndham (always known as 'Binks') were born. In later years, on a family holiday at Salcombe, Graham Harding indulged another of his great pleasures. In the harbour he saw a J-class yacht, *Iverna,* which had been converted to a houseboat. She belonged to Mr Cottle of C. T. Bowring (whose son Ronnie Cottle was to become marine managing-director of C. T. Bowring). Built at the turn of the century, she had earned a good reputation as a racer: one summer, racing against Kaiser Wilhelm's yacht *Meteor*, she had King Edward VII on board. Graham Harding bought her, and took holidays on board when he could spare the time.

At the end of the First World War, Graham Harding expanded the London office of Toplis and Harding (he had himself become a subscribing member of Lloyd's in 1917). The office was moved in 1919 from Cannon Street to 28 Old Jewry. There were two partnerships in London. Graham Harding was sole partner of Toplis and Harding (Assessing Department), which had eight salaried assessors, among them F. H. Rogers and A. J. Campbell. Francis Rogers was appointed a salaried partner in 1920 (with 15 per cent of the profits, the remainder going to Graham Harding: Rogers' share was soon increased to 20 per cent, and then, from 1921, to 48 per cent). A. J. Campbell was later to become senior partner of the Paris office. The second London partnership in 1919 was Toplis and Harding (Estate Departments 1 and 2), in which Graham Harding and Humphrey Russell were co-partners (Harding receiving one-third of the profits and Russell two-thirds). Graham Harding was also in partnership in Manchester with William Burkinshaw in the firm that was to become Toplis and Harding (Northern) Limited; but to add to the complexity, Humphrey Russell also had an interest in the Estate Department of Toplis and Harding in Manchester, sharing the profits 50/50 with Graham Harding. These tortuous arrangements were to puzzle the auditors, and indeed the future partners, for many years.

In 1918 Graham Harding had made a further journey to the United States on behalf of Lloyd's and Cuthbert Heath. On that visit, in line with his expansionist ideas, he determined to have permanent representation for Toplis and Harding in that country. This he achieved in 1920, opening offices in New York, Chicago and San Francisco.

It was on his Egyptian honeymoon that Graham Harding decided to open offices in the Middle East, which he did in 1921. This was the beginning of the Toplis and Harding offices in Alexandria, Cairo and Port Said. These were later to be managed by and in association with the local firm of Farrell, Ajus and Daniel Ghazarian. Another office was opened in Constantinople (now Istanbul). A second office in Turkey was opened in Smyrna (now Izmir) in 1922, largely as a satellite of the Constantinople office to cope with the insurance aftermath of the disastrous Smyrna conflagration when, at the end of the Greco-Turkish War, during which the Turks recovered Smyrna from Greek occupation, the city was virtually razed by fire. *The Times* reported that in late October 1922

> The whole city is one mass of ashes and tottering walls. The part destroyed by the fire was essentially the business part of the town – the warehouses containing imported goods and produce ready to be exported and the houses occupied by Europeans. Approximately 600 acres of buildings have been laid low by the fire; and the losses are estimated at £30 million.

The foreign residents, most of whom had lost everything, were leaving. Clearly it was good business to have a reputable representative of Toplis and Harding on the spot to assess the precise apportionment of compensation.

Still more European offices were opened in 1921, at Brussels, Antwerp, Marseilles, Milan (for Italy: a Genoa office was added in 1922) and Piraeus (for Greece). The Paris office also expanded significantly in these years: truly Graham Harding was a pan-European ahead of his time. But his interests were worldwide, for in 1921 also he added an office in St Louis to his American network, and expanded from the United States into Canada, with an office in Montreal. He also opened an office in Shanghai. All these were his personal ventures, conducted in the name of Toplis and Harding but independent of the London partnership.

Perhaps the crisis that gradually swept over the London partnership in 1926 owed something to its senior partner's enthusiasm for overseas interests. There was much instability in British society and in the City that year (the General Strike took place in May). At Old Jewry, there was uncertainty as to how to proceed, as the year's profits of the 'Assessing Department' (which had been over £6000 in 1921) declined to a little more than £1000. A firm of independent accountants (Deloitte, Plender, Griffiths) were invited to examine the books. As a result of its report, the various partnerships were rationalized. The auctioneering and valuation side of the business (the 'Estates Department') was hived off into a separate entity, as Toplis Harding and Russell. From this point, Toplis and Harding was to be solely occupied in the growing profession of loss adjusting.

At the same time, there were changes in the constitution of Toplis and Harding in the United States. From his long association with the insurance business in Chicago, dating back to 1910 when he had first visited as representative of Cuthbert Heath, Graham Harding was on terms of warm friendship with many of its leaders. Soon after the

Graham Harding.

First World War, Charles Wagner (who had been insurance risk manager for Armours, a leading meat packer) and Henry Glidden (claims manager for the Chicago broker with close associations with Lloyd's of London, Rollins Burdick Hunter) had gone into partnership in their own loss adjusting business, Wagner & Glidden Incorporated.

By 1927 Graham Harding had set up three companies in the United States. They were Toplis and Harding Incorporated New York, Toplis and Harding Incorporated Illinois and Toplis and Harding Incorporated California, and they became known jointly as 'The Toplis and Harding Corporations'. This was done independently of the London partners of Toplis and Harding, though with their full

44

knowledge. There was a feeling in London that if Graham Harding wanted to indulge his overseas ventures, then there was no way of stopping him; but his home partners saw themselves as being firmly established in the City of London, and preferred to operate from there. Graham Harding, on the other hand, enjoyed travelling and particularly enjoyed the excitement of life in the New World.

Henry Glidden was now sole proprietor of Wagner and Glidden. Harding and Glidden determined to merge their firms. On 16 September 1927 they made an agreement to this effect. The new joint Home office was based in Chicago but incorporated in Delaware with an issued capital of $25,000, the shares to be held in equal proportions by Glidden and Harding. The issued capital of the three Toplis and Harding companies in the USA would be increased to a total of $50,000, to be registered equally between Glidden and Harding.

Graham Harding signed it in Chicago, but Henry Glidden came to London and signed the agreement at 28 Old Jewry, witnessed by Stanley Leftwich (no doubt because Graham Harding wanted his London office to be fully apprised of what was going on). Leftwich was not yet a partner of the London firm, but he had been its cashier for seven years.

The assets of Graham Harding's Toplis and Harding Corporations in America were independently valued at $54,697, and the value placed on Wagner and Glidden was $25,418. Glidden paid over to Harding half the difference, so that they would own equal shares in the reconstituted firm. Glidden was to be permitted to draw a salary of $48,841 per annum, and Harding would receive $18,000 per annum provided the profits were adequate.

A holding company was formed to own all the capital stock of Wagner and Glidden and the Toplis Corporations in the United States. This company, the Inspection Company of America, registered in Delaware, was entirely owned by Graham Harding, Henry Glidden and A. T. Persson of Chicago (Alfred Theodore Persson was later to become chairman). In October 1937 there was a further technical reorganization of the firm, by which its title was changed to Wagner and Glidden Inc., its capital stock increased from $1000 to $50,000, and the stock holdings divided in the proportions: Graham Harding 25 per cent, Henry Glidden 25 per cent, A. T. Persson 25 per cent and other employee stockholders 25 per cent. There was also to be a further new Delaware Corporation formed entitled Toplis and Harding Inc. Eventually the firm became Toplis and Harding, Wagner and Glidden Inc., of Chicago. This firm rapidly expanded until it had offices in New York, Detroit, Boston, New Orleans,

Los Angeles, San Francisco, Seattle, Tampa, Jacksonville, Baltimore, Houston and Portland.

Henry Glidden's first lieutenant, Alfred Theodore Persson, was known as Alf – a tall, impressive Swedish American, everything about him was large. He was one of the most respected insurance men in the USA. He came to London frequently. The first time he came over, in the early thirties, he arrived in a cold February wearing what he thought was high fashion – a huge overcoat in a loud black-and-white hounds-tooth. Graham Harding took one look at it, and when it was time to go to Lloyd's, said firmly: 'We shan't need our overcoats . . .' and led the way into the street, tight-lipped. Persson delighted to recall that he nearly froze to death.

Mr Luttrell ran the New York office. He too came up against the City of London's dress regulations, when he arrived for the formal opening by King George V of the new building of Lloyd's in Leadenhall Street in 1925 wearing brown shoes. (History was reversed in 1960 when Wyndham Harding, attending a board meeting in Chicago, arrived at Persson's office in brown suede shoes, having inadvertently left his black shoes in a New York hotel room. It pleased Persson to insist on walking his guest round to the nearest shop to be properly shod.)

Alf Persson (left) and Norbert Tierney, with their wives.

Both Persson and his deputy, Norbert J. Tierney, were fastidious dressers. The Chicago office maintained a severe dress code, and it was not until the 1970s that the tradition of dark suit, white shirt and hat was relaxed.

Persson concentrated on property, and Tierney on liability claims (known as casualty in the USA). It was Persson who brought the business to prominence. While Persson was large, Tierney was very small and very tough. He had come up the hard way, from a large Irish family and had all the impishness that that background suggests. As a 'cub adjuster' he had worked in the Chicago of Al Capone, investigating and reporting on cases involving bootlegging (selling liquor during the time of prohibition) and arson.

Postwar, the Chicago office (which was appointed to the Lloyd's Agency in 1951) expanded within the Board of Trade building, but had its own entrance on Jackson Boulevard. The office was on the 25th floor in 1950; but about four years later expansion caused them to move down to grandiose offices in the Corn Exchange on the mezzanine or first floor. Here there was a wide sweeping staircase, a lavish office for Persson looking onto the street, smaller offices round the sides and a big open-plan central space where the junior adjusters sat, monitored from his office by the eagle-eye of Norbert Tierney whose desk faced the door, which was always open so that he could see what was going on.

Alf Persson was a church-goer, a serious and careful man. Tierney lived 'high on the hog'. In London, Persson would stay at Grosvenor House but use buses and tubes. Tierney would stay in a suite at the Ritz, and hire a big chauffeur-driven limousine. His brother C. W. Tierney also joined the office; a qualified lawyer, very clever with a wicked sense of humour, he dealt with the legal liability claims. The other character of those days was Tom Crowley sen., who ran the Detroit office and was a small fireball of a man. In the early 1950s A. T. Persson jun. (Ted) was sent by his father to London, where he joined C. E. Heath & Co. and later J. H. Minet & Co., for whom he broked claims in the London market.

The Detroit office was in the post-war years to take charge of the Toplis and Harding operations in Canada, which had before the war been directly responsible to Graham Harding in London. But the Montreal office was not financially viable and it was agreed that it should be controlled from the US. For some years it was nominally run from Chicago, but that office necessarily concentrated on its own work; it was not until the 1960s that Tom Crowley despatched Richard W. Gallandt to open up a Toplis and Harding office in Toronto.

In 1965 Alf Persson's son A. T. P. Persson jun., known as Ted, became President (Chief Executive) of Toplis and Harding Inc., with Alf Persson remaining as Chairman and Norbert Tierney as Vice-Chairman. Eventually Alf Persson suffered a stroke, but in the following year, though much handicapped, visited London and indomitably toured the market. Ted Persson was also very familiar with London, having trained in the market at Lloyd's, working as a broker in the Room. He ruled the Chicago office well, and became as respected as his distinguished father, on whose retirement Norbert Tierney became Chairman.

In the thirties the Los Angeles office, which had been opened by Vince Bledsoe in 1921, dealt with some of the more exotic risks that were presented in the great days of Hollywood as the home of the glamorous film industry. There was no shortage of film stars earning substantial wealth, and no shortage either of light-fingered thieves eager to relieve them of it. The records of the Los Angeles office of Toplis and Harding Inc. contain some fascinating glimpses of the tinsel-town lifestyle.

In an August weekend in 1932, for example, Zeppo Marx (one of the Marx brothers) returned with his wife from their Malibu beach cottage to discover that they had been robbed of $37,600 jewellery 'and $10 cash'. Toplis and Harding put out a reward offer of $2500. Apparently Zeppo did recover some of the jewellery, but he was unlucky: it was stolen again during another break-in nine months later.

The Marx Brothers with Zeppo on the left.

In 1933 Carole Lombard lost a star sapphire ring while at the Paramount studio: Toplis and Harding offered a reward of $1500. Whether or not she recovered the ring is not recorded.

Carole Lombard.

Sometimes the entries in the Toplis and Harding book of Hollywood press cuttings would form a good basis for a film (or at least a B feature). One personal ad reads: 'MARTHA. I want proof on ice cream deal. Phone in a.m.' No doubt a hundred scriptwriters could work that up into a gripping drama, but there is no clue as to what information Martha was offering, and for how much, and whether stolen property was recovered as a result.

Eventually one of the jewellery thieves was caught, in part through the vigilance of the Toplis and Harding office. A letter is on file dated 10 October 1935 from the Chief of Police, Los Angeles, to his opposite number in San Francisco. It reads:

> From July 1934 to June 1935, we had a daylight burglar operating in the exclusive residential district of this city. This suspect was looting the better class of homes, taking jewelry, silverware and money. Investigating officers of this department were unable to determine where the loot was being sold. In June 1935 some of the silver showed up in the pawnshops of your city. Through the alertness of your Lieut Sam Miller in charge of the Pawnshop Detail and his men, the property was identified through the co-operation of Mr Philip Gaynor, Insurance Adjuster of your city, and Mr V. E. Bledsoe of the Toplis and Harding Co. of this city. Subsequently officers of your Pawnshop Detail arrested Daniel W. Mercer in your city. Your officers, upon searching Mr Mercer's house, found a large quantity of stolen loot consisting of silverware, jewelry and rugs. Through the splendid co-operation of Charles Dulles, Captain of Inspectors, and his detailing Lieut Sam Miller and Inspector Gable to this city, these officers arrived in Los Angeles via automobile with all the loot recovered in your city and communicated with this department and gave us information which led to the arrest of Walter N. Deutsch, an ex-convict, and the daylight burglar long wanted in this city.
>
> The arrest of Deutsch here resulted in the recovery of thousands of dollars worth of stolen loot. A final investigation cleared approximately one hundred burglaries in this city and a successful prosecution of Deutsch here. Upon a plea of guilty to three counts of Burglary and three counts of Receiving Stolen Property, he was sentenced to prison for from twenty-five to sixty-five years, which practically means life imprisonment for him.

Not all the insurance problems in Los Angeles were quite so dramatic, though many have an historic interest. Lloyd's took on some unusual risks; for example, it was reported in 1933 that:

> A $50,000 figure is sometimes called a 'nice round figure', but in the case of Bette Davis, youthful cinema star, it is just the opposite.
>
> Her figure is slim and her build petite and Warner Brothers believe it is worth $50,000 at the box office.
>
> They have applied to Lloyd's of London for a $50,000 policy protecting the studio against the possibility that Miss Davis may get fat. . . .
>
> Lloyd's will be safeguarded, however, by a provision which permits (the company) to put Bette on a diet the moment she reaches 115 pounds, if she does. Since Bette has never in her life weighed more

Bette Davis.

than 108, the risk is considered negligible and the premium may not be great.

In the next year, another Hollywood star made the headlines through insurance. And a dramatic headline it was:

17 BRITISH LORDS AND EARLS SHARE $25,000 RISK

Seventeen Lords and Earls are among the 488 prominent Britishers who have insured 6-year-old Shirley Temple against accident.

Shirley received her $25,000 policy yesterday from an English company with which her parents, Mr & Mrs George F. Temple, insured her because no company in this country will write a policy for any considerable sum on a child.

In case Shirley should meet a violent death, the 488 individual underwriters would divide the $25,000 loss pro rata. The cost of the policy is comparatively small, the annual premium being $350.

One clause of the policy emphatically sets forth that the insured must not take up arms in warfare and another says that payment shall be cancelled if Shirley meets death or injury while intoxicated.

Shirley Temple (aged 6).

It is scarcely surprising that Lloyd's became so highly respected in Hollywood that Twentieth Century Fox announced that they were planning a film, possibly starring Ronald Colman (the great heart-throb of the day, and so a natural to play a loss adjuster . . .), to be called 'Lloyd's of London'.

The Lloyd's agency in Los Angeles came to Toplis and Harding Inc. through a merger with Best & Co., a firm founded by A. Lester Best and specialising in cargo surveying and appraising, and run after Best's death by Frank Niner. In the thirties, Toplis and Harding Inc. was most respected for its international links, while its associated company Wagner & Glidden specialized in fire claims.

If Lloyd's had an easy risk in the young Shirley Temple, the underwriters were less fortunate with a film directed in 1937 by Hal Roach. A Hollywood gossip columnist wrote that year:

> Hal Roach isn't worrying, despite the fact that he's had to halt production on 'Merrily We Live', with the highest price cast he ever assembled, because every member of said cast, not to mention Director Norman McLeod and Cameraman Norbert Brodine, is down with the flu. Mr Roach is sorry the folks are sick but it isn't costing him a cent.
>
> Last Friday, Mr Roach took out a blanket health policy with Lloyd's. About ten minutes after the policy was okayed, Constance Bennett collapsed. Since then, the distinguished array has been going down like dominoes. Brian Aherne held out until yesterday but he had to quit and reached bed just one jump ahead of McLeod and Brodine.

There was a pleasantly family atmosphere about the Los Angeles office, for Vince Bledsoe's secretary Fanchon Roberts married her boss's assistant, Art Eggenberger, who succeeded him as a director and Vice-President of Toplis and Harding Inc. He specialized in motion picture cast losses. Another long-serving member of staff was Lucy Enos.

Finally, pasted into the cuttings book of Toplis Harding Inc. Los Angeles is a poem published in 1940 in the journal of the NAIIA, and written by W. E. Severance.

THE CLAIM ADJUSTER

When the Doomsday Book is finished
And man's work on earth is through,
There will come before St Peter
A depressed and motley crew.

They will be the claim adjusters,
And each sinner will request
That he may receive a passport
To the kingdom of the blest.

Gone will be the scintillation
From each troubled heart and eye,
While they scrutinize their conscience
For some worthy alibi.

And St Peter will determine
What they did both night and day,
And in reaching a decision
I predict that he will say:

'You were energetic workers
And I'd grant you rest and peace,
But you all were too ambitious
Getting names on a release.'

'You have settled scores of cases,
Which adjusters should not do;
Litigation helps the lawyers –
Sorry boys, it's hell for you.'

The association of Toplis and Harding with Hollywood was to continue into the post-war era. The daughter of the head of the New York office, Theodore Holm, became the distinguished actress Celeste Holm. Theo Holm made an immense success of the marine side of the business (the New York office held the Lloyd's Agency from 1933 and also that of the Institute of London Underwriters). Holm's successor was Rolf V. Corsgreen, who controlled the agency for many years; his successor was Robert K. Tisdall.

6. The Fire Business

IN 1933, the Manchester office of Toplis and Harding, headed by William Burkinshaw, participated with William Charles Crocker (who described it in detail in his book *Far from Humdrum*) in the 'Fire Conspiracy' case, a classic of criminal arson. In 1931 the insurance world noticed that an unusual number of claims were being made, and paid, in relation to shops and warehouses that had caught fire in various parts of London and Manchester. The claims were being made on behalf of the assured by Leopold Harris, an assessor. Several fire offices used the services of an adjuster named A. J. Loughborough Ball. In each case Ball agreed the claim. Since the insurance world was afflicted by growing doubts about the genuineness of these conflagrations, and by growing losses from the large sums being paid out, William Charles Crocker was commissioned by the general manager of the Sun Insurance Company, and by a group of senior Lloyd's members, to investigate.

Gradually he built up a dossier, case by case. The corroborative evidence came from many points of detail. As one example, it was noticed after one fire that undamaged bundles of silks were in double wrappers. The outer wrappers were undamaged, but the inner wrappers showed signs of smoke and water damage, indicating that the contents had been in a previous fire and were now being used as what the trade called 'old soldiers' to add to the quantity of contents due for destruction in a new blaze.

The Manchester office of Toplis and Harding was brought in when on 9 September 1931 there was a fire at 27 York Street, Manchester, in the premises of Acevose Silks (a company, financed by Leopold Harris, that had previously suffered losses in a fire at its London premises in Staining Lane). The floor below was occupied by a new firm of silk merchants, Richard Glen & Co. The fire virtually gutted the building. Acevose Silks had thoughtfully insured the stock for £35,000, with an additional £15,000 for consequential loss. On the stock loss, the claim went through the crooked system and was paid. On the consequential loss, an honest assessor refused flatly to countenance any claim. Then the claim came in for the Richard Glen losses. It was referred to the Manchester office of Toplis and Harding. Burkinshaw, advised by Graham Harding, after a word with his good friend Crocker, refused to agree to any payment. The claim was not pressed. Eventually the conspirators were arrested, and at the Old Bailey in August 1933 Leopold Harris was sentenced to 14 years in gaol and his associates to lesser terms.

The case was made even more dramatic when it was finally revealed that the Chief of the London Salvage Corps, the private brigade financed by the insurance companies, was himself part of the conspiracy. He was eventually arrested, charged, and given four years penal servitude. Following the successful conclusion of the case, a number of senior Lloyd's brokers (among them M. W. Drysdale, afterwards Sir Matthew and Chairman of Lloyd's) sent a letter to Graham Harding recording their

> great appreciation, not only of the skill displayed by Mr Burkinshaw in his ordinary capacity as an assessor, but also of his quite remarkable initiative and untiring efforts which, in a great measure, have contributed to the disclosure of the incendiary schemes of these particular criminals, and in the larger issue to the final defeat of the greatest conspiracy ever known in the history of Fire Insurance in this country.

In 1935 Graham Harding personally took charge of the adjustment following the great fire in London Docklands which virtually destroyed Colonial Wharf. On 26 September 1935 the business pages of *The Times* carried a company report concerning Colonial Wharves Ltd of Wapping, which had become a public company in the previous year. During the year, said the report, a new warehouse had been completed 'and is almost full of goods stored by customers'. A further warehouse was under construction. This good news became heavily ironical, because by the time the newspaper was on the streets, the new warehouse was an inferno and the London Fire Brigade (using new Massey Harris water cannon for the first time from the river) was battling to control a fire that threatened to emulate the terrible devastation caused to London's docklands by the Tooley Street fire 70 years earlier. *The Times* reported:

> The great riverside fire . . . at Wapping continued throughout yesterday, casting over a wide area a dense pall of thick black smoke from which flames shot out at intervals. . . . The efforts of the firemen were largely concentrated on keeping the fire within the one warehouse in which it had started . . .

Telegraphic Address
LLOYD'S,
LONDON.

Telephone
AVENUE 7100.

LLOYD'S,
LONDON, E.C.3.

10th January, 1935.

Graham Harding, Esq.,
Messrs. Toplis & Harding,
28, Old Jewry, E.C. 2.

Dear Sir,

                Re: E.Wolfe t/a Richard Glen & Company,
                    27, York St., Manchester.

           In reference to the prolonged investigation by
your Manchester office, of the bogus claim put forward in 1931
by this member of the Leopold Harris gang of incendiaries, which
has just recently been brought to so successful a conclusion,
we desire to place on record our great appreciation, not only
of the skill displayed by Mr. Burkinshaw in his ordinary capacity
as an assessor, but also of his quite remarkable initiative and
untiring efforts which, in a great measure, have contributed to
the disclosure of the incendiary schemes of these particular
criminals, and in the larger issue to the final defeat of the
greatest conspiracy ever known in the history of Fire insurance
in this country.

           We should feel greatly obliged if you would be so
good as to convey these sentiments to Mr. Burkinshaw on our
behalf, together with a request that he will accept for himself
the amount which he has collected for us, as a slight token of
our thanks to him personally for his splendid work.

                             Yours faithfully,

Letter to Graham Harding from senior members of Lloyd's following the fire-raisers' case, 1935.

57

Firemen with half a lifetime's experience had never seen a fire so stubborn. The scene was grotesque. The wind now blew from the south, forcing great volumes of black smoke across and down into Wapping High Street and wrapping the whole of the affected sector in a dense fog. . . .

On the riverside the scene of ruin was even more complete. Most of the riverside wall had fallen, and in the low state of the tide its wreckage lay on the mud mixed with that of the giant crane which fell on Wednesday night, a smashed lighter or two, and masses of crude rubber, all of which burned continuously like a vast bonfire.

The fire was contained within a few days by the efforts of the London Fire Brigade, which earned much praise. The damage to the building was estimated at £42,000, and the loss of commodities £258,000, a total of £300,000. The principal damage was to rubber, while tea, copper, spelter (zinc) and wines were also affected. Insurances on the commodities were mostly on 'floating policies'. While most of the loss fell on the fire insurance companies and non-marine underwriting syndicates, some of the rubber (the value of which was over £100,000) was covered by marine policies under 'warehouse to warehouse' clauses.

Graham Harding and his colleagues had to resolve this complicated scenario. The London Fire Brigade also came out of the business well, since it had prevented the fire from reaching a neighbouring warehouse valued at £60,000, and four other warehouses on the west side of Colonial Wharf which held stocks of tea valued at £250,000 – one of these warehouses suffered some water damage, but the others were unscathed.

Just under a year later, in December 1936, Graham Harding dealt with the aftermath of the fire that destroyed Crystal Palace, the famous structure designed by the Duke of Devonshire's gardener, afterwards Sir Joseph Paxton, to house the Great Exhibition of 1851 in Hyde Park, and subsequently rebuilt in an enlarged form at Sydenham in South London. The fire started in an office, and was first noticed at about 7.30 pm on 30 November. An orchestra was rehearsing in part of the building, and at first there seemed to be no great danger (there had been three fires, all quickly contained, while the Crystal Palace was at Sydenham). But there was a fresh wind and it caught the flames, which took a strong hold before the Fire Brigade could gain control. By 10.30 that evening more than two-thirds of the great building was a flaring mass of ruins on the ground, a wreckage of tangled girders and molten glass. The glow was visible in the sky as far as Brighton, and sightseers flocked to watch the sight (which further handicapped the fire-fighting). The building covered an area of 1400 ft by 1000 ft, and had been used as showrooms, studios (including Baird's television studios), workshops, offices and stores.

The managing-director of the Crystal Palace company (which managed the building on behalf of trustees), Sir Henry Buckland, said that while it had cost £1,350,000 to build, its replacement cost would be between £4 million and £5 million. It was insured for £110,000, and the organ was separately insured for £10,000. Insurances on the contents – mainly catering and exhibition equipment – totalled a further £70,000. The low figure was based on the fact that when the building had been bought from the South Kensington Great Exhibition organizers for the nation, in 1911, the price paid was £200,000 (and most of that was attributable to the cost of the Sydenham site).

On the instructions of the leading insurer, Cuthbert Heath of Lloyd's, Graham Harding was one of the first on the scene on the day after the fire, acting on behalf of Lloyd's. His report was one of the shortest he ever wrote: it was on a half-sheet of paper. There

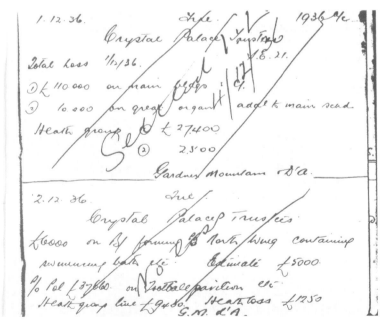

Entry in the underwriters' book of C. E. Heath, showing that the claim of the Trustees of the Crystal Palace was settled four days after the fire.

was no question but that the Crystal Palace was a total loss: nothing was recoverable. Harding recommended that the claim should be paid in full. Exactly one week after the fire the Crystal Palace trustees received a cheque from Lloyd's underwriters for £120,000, being £110,000 for the insurances effected on the structure, and £10,000 for

Searching the wreckage after the Crystal Palace fire.

the insurances for the organ. It can scarcely have given the trustees any joy.

It was not, however, strictly true that nothing survived. In the midst of the Crystal Palace there had been an aquarium, filled with goldfish. For a day or two after the fire, they had been written off as 'missing, believed boiled'. Then they were found, still swimming around, though discoloured.

A man's hair, in comparable circumstances, would have turned white [commented *The Times*]; the goldfish have gone black all over. They cannot be blamed for doing so. They are not the first to be forced off the gold standard by circumstances, and they may rest assured that no political significance will be attached to their choice of a new livery.

Crystal Palace after the fire.

61

7. War and Aftermath

ON 3 September 1939 Britain declared war on Hitler's Germany which, it was at last realized, was intent upon aggression in Europe. At Toplis and Harding, the partners in London were left without the senior partner. In the late thirties Graham Harding had been spending more and more time in Switzerland on his doctor's orders, since the mountain climate relieved his breathing problems. Now he was isolated in Lenzerheide, near Chur and unable to return. He could only communicate with London by mail. Nevertheless, while living in a country that remained neutral in the conflict, he did what he could for the British war effort, helping a number of British and American servicemen who escaped into Switzerland on their way back to the UK. By chance one of the American airmen had been on the staff of Rollins Burdick and, having been shot down while on a bombing raid over Germany, had escaped to Switzerland and successfully sought out his company's old business associate, who duly helped him.

In London, as the younger men went to war, the older and those less fit were left to keep the business going. In the thirties assessing had been a somewhat buccaneering and individualistic way of life: at least one of its practitioners (not in T and H) had gone too far and found himself on the wrong side of the law. At first, in 1939, it was assumed that war would be as it had been a quarter of a century earlier; it would be waged outside the United Kingdom. That was certainly the view of the British Government. It was assumed that if war came, the schemes used in 1914–18 would cover all likely eventualities; insurance companies, and Lloyd's, acting as Government agents, would issue policies against damage by aircraft or bombardment (of the sort whose consequences Graham Harding had dealt with in the north-east of England in 1916). Following the heavy bombing by the Italians in Abyssinia, and by German aircraft during the Spanish Civil War, successive Presidents of the Board of Trade gave it as the official view that there could be no official compensation for air-raid damage.

There was increasing public pressure for insurance schemes to be introduced, and in consequence the need for assessment and adjustment of claims. At first, with the War Risks Insurance Act of 1939, there was compulsory registration of commodities only. It was laid down that the staff of the Superintending Valuer of the Board of Inland Revenue would assess claims, and pass them to the Board of Trade: this despite the fact that District Valuers had virtually no experience of averaging, which would be required by the Commodities Scheme. It was realized that there might not be enough staff to cope, and senior members in the principal firms of assessors were notified that they might be needed to help.

It was fortunate that, for the first year of the war, there was no bombing of British cities. The civil service and the assessing community moved slowly towards formulating some practical scheme. The main difficulty was that assessors were so individualistic that while they were very well aware of each other's activities, they saw each other as rivals and had no common professional body to speak for them as a group. The pressure of events brought them together. On the night of 7 September 1940 there was a massive bombing raid on London; raids continued for two months. The damage was formidable. Firms of assessors were allocated to areas, and allowed (uniquely) to photograph the damage. The Board of Trade proposed a scale of fees requiring assessors to determine how many hours they devoted to each claim, and charge accordingly. The volume of work soon became so great that such a system was impracticable.

The need for the profession to speak with a single voice brought the rivals together. On 21 December 1940 eight leading London assessors met for luncheon at the Holborn Restaurant. At that meeting they formed The Fire Loss Adjusters' Association. There was evidently no discussion of the use of what was then the American term 'adjuster', rather than 'assessor'; it has been said that the intention was to avoid confusion with other types of assessors, such as legal and income tax assessors. (G. T. H. Sharp: *A Profession Emerges, History of the Loss Adjusting Profession*, Part II, 1986.)

One of the older assessors present had good reason to be aware of the consequences of air attack. He was Col. Cuthbert Buckle, head of the firm of Ellis and Buckle, who had in 1917–19 been Air Defence Commander of London Air Defences. The Holborn meeting elected as Chairman the respected J. McMullen Brooks of Howell and Brooks. The Honorary Secretary was to be James Perry of Toplis and Harding. Perry, having worked for the firm for 20 years, had became a partner earlier that year, together with Ninian Hawken, Brian Leftwich and Patrick Harding. The last three were now away at the war, so that the London office was being run by Perry with his contemporary Stanley Leftwich; they had been joined in the office at Old Jewry by Arthur Campbell, head of the Paris office, who had escaped with difficulty after the fall of France that summer. Another pillar of the wartime office was William Henry Morse. Before the war he had been Senior Commissionaire, a formidable figure. He

James Perry of Toplis and Harding, first Secretary of the Fire Loss Adjusters' Association.

64

had also acted as butler for Graham Harding's office lunches, going over to fetch the food (always the same) from Pimm's in Poultry. He became an adjuster during the war, and was entirely competent in handling simple jobs. However, report writing was a great effort for him, and his desk was pitted with cigarette burns for he would lodge his non-filter cigarette upright on the desk as he sought for a word, and it would often smoulder down to the wood.

Perry provided the administrative drive to found what was to become the professional institution for British loss adjusters, ably seconded by his secretary Miss Moore and, from 1945, the indomitable Mrs Helen Marr as the association's part-time Assistant Secretary. The need to get the organization in place is illustrated by the speed with which it was done. Following the Saturday luncheon, a second meeting was held on the next Monday in the offices of Toplis and Harding, when it was agreed to invite other London and provincial members to join.

An office was established on the first floor of the Toplis and Harding office at 28 Old Jewry; and because, owing to wartime conditions, a telephone could not be installed for some months, Toplis and Harding allowed its own telephone to be used. Within a few months, a deputation from the association was meeting a representative of the Board of Trade to discuss an alternative scale of payment for war damage work. The first General Meeting of the association was held at the Connaught Rooms on 6 February 1942, and was followed by a luncheon attended by the Lord Mayor of London and the Sheriff, other official representatives and, from the world of insurance, the Chairman of the British Insurance Association, the Chairman of Lloyd's Fire and Non-Marine Association, the President of the Chartered Insurance Institute, the President of the Corporation of Insurance Brokers and the Chairman of the Average Adjusters' Association.

The authoritative welcome thus given to the new association demonstrated that it was recognized as a necessary body to represent a profession; it also reflected James Perry's persuasiveness and his secretary's administrative skills, which were to be demonstrated annually in the following years by the organization of a dinner that was generally regarded as one of the high-spots of the social year in the insurance world. (In 1961, just 21 years after its foundation, the association was granted a Royal Charter as the Chartered Institute of Loss Adjusters.)

The office in Old Jewry was made available to members of the association on those occasions when their own offices and records were destroyed in the continuing blitz on London. Sadly, on Friday

6 October 1944 a V-bomb destroyed that office also, and with it almost all the past partnership records and mementoes of Toplis and Harding. An office was taken in Cornhill, where in the last year of the war the remaining partners began to rebuild a business from the rubble of the past. That this was done speedily and efficiently was largely due to Freddie Gould, a gentle kindly bachelor and much respected accident loss adjuster.

The office at 28 Old Jewry following its destruction by a V-bomb, 6 October 1944.

Gradually the Toplis and Harding office was reconstructed at 78 Cornhill, to which the younger partners returned after war service. One chose not to come back: Patrick Harding, elder son of Graham Harding, decided in 1946 that the City was not the life for him, and resigned from the partnership to make his life elsewhere. Graham Harding's younger son, Wyndham Harding, did however join the firm. Stanley Leftwich had seen the business through the war, but had been crushed by the death in June 1942 of his son Brian Leftwich, who was lost when the Red Cross ship in which he was returning home after being wounded in action was torpedoed. In 1947 there was a difference of opinion between the partners who had remained during the war, and those now returning from war service; and in that year Stanley Leftwich chose to retire, in circumstances that were not harmonious. Two new partners were introduced: Freddie Gould, and Dudley Strevens (who was the son-in-law of Stanley Leftwich).

In 1947 there returned to the partnership from the war the man who was more than any other to lead it to success in the next 20 years: Ninian Hawken. Hawken went into the Army on the outbreak of war. He joined the 1/7th Queen's (Royal Surrey) Regiment, and soon saw action in Northern France. In May 1940, during the British retreat to Dunkirk, he was a Second Lieutenant in charge of a party ordered to destroy coal barges on the canal at La Bresse. Under considerable enemy fire, he and his group managed to destroy 250 barges; he was awarded the Military Cross for his achievement. On 15 March 1941, while stationed in Kent, he married at Hale parish church near Farnham in Surrey. His bride was Elizabeth Margaret Alinora Browning, a descendant of a collateral branch of the family of the poets Robert and Elizabeth Barrett Browning.

But then the war claimed him again. As a Captain in General Montgomery's Eighth Army in North Africa he was active in the early stages of the Battle of Alamein in October 1942. Although wounded, he organized the withdrawal of remnants of platoons to a nearby wadi where they re-formed; he then led them back into action. By the next year he had been promoted Major, was in the Battle of Medenine, and was with the British troops when the Germans surrendered Tunis in May 1943. He went on with the war in Italy, where he was again wounded and then invalided out of the army. One of his most famous decisions was to put his own Colonel under arrest at a critical moment, a bold act that was later vindicated by a military tribunal. Ninian Hawken therefore returned to Toplis and Harding in 1947 after a most distinguished war.

As the office returned to normal and began to pick up its inter-national links which had been broken by the war, it was decided to improve morale by holding an annual staff night out. The first was rather austere – high tea at Fullers in Chancery Lane, with fish and chips, followed by a visit to a play put on by the Lloyd's Amateur Dramatic Society. In the second year the occasion became more lively, with drinks, and then a visit to one of the great American musicals at Drury Lane. The office took a row of the dress circle. The night out became convivial, and at one point – bored with some sentimental nonsense between hero and heroine – the distinguished figure of one of the older partners, Harold Anning, rose unsteadily to his feet and pointing at the stage, boomed: 'Enough of this bunny-cuddling! Get on with the story!' The staff annual get-together survived this unscheduled intervention, and in later years became a dinner-dance at the Connaught Rooms, to which overseas guests were welcomed. One year there was a Chinese guest; with good intentions, one partner sent his secretary to a local Chinese restaurant to obtain a welcome in phonetic Chinese. He duly learnt and recited it, but was greeted by a blank Chinese incomprehension. It was the wrong variant of Chinese.

On 29 May 1949 Graham Harding died at Chur, Switzerland. He was 70. In 1895 he had become a pupil of his father in the family firm of loss adjusters in the City of London: fifteen years later he had become principal partner of Toplis and Harding on his father's premature death. Through personality, effectiveness and flair he had almost single-handed created a distinguished business, reputable and renowned internationally; he was as well known and respected in the United States and Canada as he was in London. He had been an annual subscriber to Lloyd's from 1917. He could have claimed to be the mainspring of Toplis and Harding throughout much of the first half of the twentieth century; his contribution to the City and his profession was to be continued by his younger son, Wyndham Harding, known to everyone as 'Binks', who joined the partnership that year. He was the fourth generation of his family to serve the firm, for a continuous period spanning more than a century.

8. Suez and Middle East Oil

IN OCTOBER 1954 Toplis and Harding opened an office in Baghdad, the capital of Iraq. The argument for it was that there the firm would be well placed to service the rapidly growing international business community attracted by the new wealth from Middle East oil and the construction industries associated with it.

On the night of 2 November 1956 three large pumping installations in the Syrian desert were seriously damaged by explosion and fire. The installations were owned by the Iraq Petroleum Company and linked to the pipeline sending oil from the Kirkuk fields to the Mediterranean outlets at Banyas and Tripoli (North Lebanon). Within a few weeks, various lengths of pipeline operated by the company in Lebanon and Jordan were similarly damaged.

Also in November 1956 a pipeline operated by the Qatar Petroleum Company was damaged by an explosion and, in the following month, an oil well operated by the same company (a parallel company to the Iraq Petroleum Company) was similarly damaged. Qatar was at that time one of the nine independent Emirates in the Arabian Gulf, in special treaty relations with the United Kingdom.

The insurance claims presented after these events were in each of the two cases in excess of £8 million. Toplis and Harding were commissioned to adjust these losses. Ninian Hawken took charge of the operation. Two years later, he produced a 'Memorandum' whose object was to report 'the results of preliminary investigations made into the causes, direct and indirect, of these events'. This 'Memorandum' runs to 397 pages and is a masterpiece of the loss adjuster's skill – packed with practical information, but tempered with humour and a reasonable cynicism.

There were some difficulties. A war was on at the time. Indeed, it did not take any great imagination to deduce that the blowing up of these pipelines might have some association with the Middle East conflict that has become known as the 'Suez campaign'. Hawken's report began with a historical 'diary' running to six pages. The outline describes the onset of the crisis. The British Government, under

Winston Churchill, had withdrawn most of its troops from the bases in the Suez Canal zone that had remained since 1945. But the Canal itself was still British-owned and operated.

In the autumn of 1955 (a few months after the 80-year-old Churchill resigned the premiership and was succeeded by Anthony Eden) the vigorous President of Egypt, Col. Nasser, had made an arms pact with Eastern Europe (Czechoslovakia) that profoundly disturbed the West, concerned that Egypt might lead the Middle East – and specifically its oil supplies – into the Russian camp.

The Americans had been about to finance a huge dam to irrigate southern Egypt, the Aswan High Dam. In July 1956 they announced that they would not provide the finance. Six days later, Col. Nasser nationalized the Suez Canal. Outraged, Britain together with France proposed to the United States that the Canal should become an international waterway. As this could only be ensured by military action, war in the Middle East drew inexorably nearer. Syria – through which country much of the pipeline ran – assured the British and US Governments in August that it would be able to protect the oil pipelines 'as long as general circumstances remained normal'. They did not remain normal for long.

The complicated political and military fencing of that autumn and winter have been described many times. The Israelis eventually launched an attack upon Jordan and then, at the end of October, in Sinai. Meanwhile the British and French announced that they would combine in military action 'to separate the combatants', Israel and Egypt. After floating around the Mediterranean for a week while political activity fermented, British and French paratroops landed at Sinai on 5 November. On the following day, the US Government having indicated that it would not support the Anglo-French action morally, let alone militarily, there was a cease-fire, after which United Nations peacekeeping forces were introduced.

The Anglo-French action at Suez would have been more credible, perhaps, if it had not been known by far too many people that there had been collusion in its preparation between the British, French and Israelis – notably at meetings outside Paris in October. It is interesting that the chronology in Ninian Hawken's report, compiled not many months afterwards, contains the significant entry for 'mid-October':

> Mysterious comings and goings between Paris and London; conversation between Ministers. Israeli personalities reported to have visited Paris.

Hawken had to try and establish who had blown up the oil installations and cut the pipelines in Syria and Qatar. It is evident that Hawken or his assistants read most of the published journalism and books published on the crisis at that time, and then set out to interview some dozens of people who were at or near the site of the damage: this involved interviews round the world, from London to Beirut and even Delhi, among local businessmen and politicians (as far as it was possible even to talk to them, in the atmosphere of recrimination and anger that pervaded the Middle East after Suez). There were also interviews with British expatriates who had been working for the oil companies, construction companies, and the local offices of (for example) BOAC, the British Overseas Airways Corporation.

Attempts were made to interview British diplomats who had been in the Middle East at the time, but this was largely fruitless. The Foreign Office eventually proposed

> to draw up a Statement of such relevant facts as are known, the disclosure of which would not be contrary to the public interest. This statement could then be produced in Court at the appropriate time, but the person producing it would not be subject to cross-examination or examination on it.

This proposal was accepted, though Hawken noted that as the British Government held a substantial shareholding in the Iraq Petroleum Company, its independence of view could not be guaranteed. In general, British Embassies abroad proved to be less than helpful, perhaps not surprisingly in the circumstances. A formal visit to the British Embassy in Baghdad

> produced no results. The Official interviewed . . . expressed surprise that any investigation was required, owing to the 'general knowledge of Syrian activities' – to use his diplomatic phrase. He remarked that the Foreign Office in London 'knew all about it' but suggested that the information the Foreign Office had was 'probably classified anyway'.

It is evident that from this point Hawken despaired of getting any help from British official representatives in the Middle East (it was significant that the 'Official' deputed to see him in Baghdad was a lowly Commercial Secretary: the Ambassador was never available). In Beirut,

> assistance from [British] Embassy officials was sought but no help was forthcoming.

71

In Beirut there were offers of information from other sources. One Syrian insurance man was asked to go to Beirut to talk, but

> refused to see anyone on learning of the purpose of the proposed interview. Said the matter was very dangerous indeed.

A well-known Lebanese businessman and politician of the time, Emile Bustani, said in an interview that in his opinion the destruction was certainly not done by the Syrian Government, which had been 'very annoyed' about the damage. He had also seen President Nasser who 'was furious – he did not want it at all – it was done by some group of fanatics and one or two Army Officers'. Subsequently Hawken discovered that Bustani had just written a book advocating the formation of Arab Development Bank, and therefore had his own reasons for the explanations. In that book, however, was this paragraph:

> Syria has already seen fit to blow up pipelines carrying Iraqi Oil, and relations between the two nations are hardly at their happiest at present.
> [Emile Bustani, *Doubts and Dynamite: The Middle East Today*, Allan Wingate, London, 1958].

Hawken felt, as he wrote, that Bustani's attitude 'is coloured by his political and commercial interests'.

One British businessman who

> has numerous contacts and family connections in the Levant, expressed the opinion that ex-Syrian Politicians and/or Military men might be found to provide evidence about the Syrian incidents. In the opinion of this businessman (who declined to have his name recorded officially) the Syrian damages were done as an act of policy, probably not by the Government as such but by the Army or Deuxième Bureau [intelligence]. The work was not that of a band of fanatics or workers but of men of power with a proper organisation.

It was necessary to make careful judgments of the bona fides of people offering information. In Beirut also Hawken met two British businessmen

> whose names were given by various people as being very knowledgeable about Syrian affairs. . . . Both promised to provide evidence of all kinds, contemporary documents and 'everything you need', *at a price*. These men, when checked on through appropriate quarters in London, turned out to be very little better than con-men and the contacts were not pursued.

Others were more reliable. One young British journalist was interviewed in London, where he was Deputy Editor of the *New Statesman*. He is described in the report as 'Aged about 27: Very intelligent. Left wing. This man has written two very readable books on the Suez and Middle East Affairs'. This was Paul Johnson (now one of Britain's leading right-wing commentators). In his book *Journey into Chaos*, MacGibbon & Kee, London, 1958, he wrote

> Of all the Middle Eastern States – including Egypt – Syria is the most savagely suspicious of 'Western Imperialism', the most acutely conscious of her hard won national sovereignty. The hatred of France, in particular, amounts to a national obsession. Syrian Army Units were instructed to blow up the I.P.C. pumping stations during the Suez crisis (a quite unnecessary operation: all the Syrians had to do to stop the flow of oil was to turn a few valves) because the government was convinced that French paratroops were about to be dropped on their heads. A senior army officer told me: 'We know for a fact that Admiral Barjot (the Deputy Commander of Operation Musketeer) had prepared a plan for the reoccupation of our country by French forces. That was why we were unable to come to Egypt's aid by attacking Israel.

A gloss was provided to this by a man described as 'a prominent Beirut businessman introduced by Lloyd's: not prepared to have his name mentioned but willing to be very helpful in other ways', who explained in an interview that

> It is probable that the destruction was ordered by the Joint Command (Syria, Jordan, Egypt). . . . Possibly Egyptians were implicated but not alone and in isolation from Syrians. Syrians seriously feared an attack by Anglo-French Forces built up in Cyprus. Mere turning off the taps would have only irritated the West: to destroy the pumping stations in an obscure manner appeared a political master stroke and prevented immediate action by England and France on the one hand and Iraq on the other. A definite military operation conceived for political ends. . . .

Some of the most significant evidence, however, came from statements elicited from four young British electrical riggers, working under contract at the pumping stations. They were tracked down back in Britain, and each independently told how they had been put into trucks by Syrian soldiers, and driven some miles from the pumping stations; on the way, they heard and saw explosions. This added yet stronger support to the accumulating accounts of what really happened.

Evidence for the reasons why it happened was assisted by the

73

friendly social relations being built up between Toplis and Harding staff in Baghdad and local professional people, so that a number of Iraqis were eventually willing to give at least informal points to likely lines of enquiry. It did no harm that Ninian Hawken never attempted to disguise his Englishness, and indeed at times parodied himself; on at least one occasion he flew into Baghdad wearing a dark City suit and a bowler hat. But he was constantly surprising his younger colleagues with curious by-ways of knowledge. Once, crossing the desert at night by taxi, he made the driver stop, took a bearing from the stars, and then demonstrated that they were going in the wrong direction. No doubt that skill had been learned with the Eighth Army in the Western Desert. Yet – despite his military gallantry – he was almost obsessively peaceable, and whatever the dangers, refused to carry a gun (though he would compromise, it was said, by carrying the tripod stand for a machine gun). He also had a fine command of language and could turn a neat phrase. In a less warlike context, he once wrote a report on the theft of jewellery from a wealthy woman in a Paris hotel. He explained that she had met a young man, and taken him to her room. 'During the ensuing nocturnal pleasantries', he wrote, the jewels vanished.

The Memorandum on the Iraq pipeline claim was delivered in little more than two years from the event. That was quick work in the circumstances. Some asked why Hawken had needed to go into such profound detail. With hindsight, it might indeed have been done more simply. But it was not in Hawken's nature to do a job without exploring every possible avenue. The task was complex, and it was impossible to weigh the value of each piece of evidence until it had been collected and assessed. By the time the Memorandum was presented, there had been a coup d'etat in Iraq: the young King Faisal II was assassinated in July 1958.

The conclusions of the Memorandum, though the evidence was far from watertight, was that the destruction of the pumping stations and the severing of the oil pipeline in Syria was the work of 'Regular Members of the Armed Forces'. There were, Hawken believed, two groups of them. One had arranged for the interruption of IPC communications and the removal of staff from the stations. The second group, probably not more than 25 commandos, had carried out the explosions, to a very compressed timetable considering the distances.

> Very considerable quantities of explosives would be needed for an operation of this sort. One informant thought about 1,000 lbs dynamite per station: this would imply the carriage of some 2 tons of demolition

equipment. But even with 25 men, this could be carried in three or four vehicles. The Syrians have no misgivings about overloading trucks, cars and jeeps. Considerable care and training would be needed to effect such an operation. However, if the idea had come to mind after the Suez Crisis broke (end-July 1956), there would have been ample time to train effective personnel.

One of Ninian Hawken's characteristics was his fairness, even when dealing with saboteurs. He felt impelled to record that he admired their skill.

> The efficiency of the operation is surprising: the alleged authors are said to boast about it. If they do so they have some justification from their point of view.

He went on to give it as his opinion that the demolition job had been commanded by the leader of Syria's Special Warfare Troops, on orders from the director of the Deuxième Bureau in Damascus. Hawken thought that the Syrian Government probably knew nothing about it beforehand, but backed it afterwards; while they had earlier given the British and French Governments assurances that the pipeline would be safe 'as long as general circumstances remain normal',

> circumstances in early November 1956 were far from normal. Israeli forces were operating in Sinai, British and French aircraft were bombing Egyptian airfields and war was in full swing (though undeclared).

This was the explanation of why the Syrians had destroyed the pumping stations instead of simply 'turning off the taps', as they could quite well have done.

> It is believed likely that the Syrian military believed (and possibly the Egyptians believed also) that the French or English or Israelis or all three would have at once invaded Syria and occupied the pipeline zone had the taps merely been turned off. Some believe that the then Iraq Government would have acted also. As destruction on a widespread scale had been done in circumstances of some obscurity, no immediate reaction came from the 'Western Powers': which was hoped would be the result. The Syrians probably believed, wrongly, that the English and French (in particular the English) had almost unlimited numbers of ships, planes, tanks, troops and especially paratroops available for operations in the Middle East at immediate notice. They had, of course, seen something of the power of British Arms in the 1939/45 War, when hundreds of thousands of British troops [among them, Major Hawken] milled around in the Middle East: little did the Syrians (or Egyptians) know of the difficulties the

75

Western Powers faced in the military sphere alone (quite apart from their political difficulties) when mounting the Port Said operation.*

It was a typically common-sense appraisal. Enquiries were continued round the world, but with the revolution in Iraq and the political trials that followed, it became more and more difficult for Toplis and Harding to operate. The first manager of the Baghdad office (in 1956) had been Ted Corby; having assisted with the pipeline enquiry, he returned to London in 1958, and was followed by Douglas Hall. His associations had been with the old regime and so on the coup d'etat it was thought wise that he should be succeeded by his newly arrived young assistant William Brown. After a year he was followed by Edwin Davies, and then Eddie Rose. The main business in those years was concerned with road building contracts, and the building of the Dukan and Derbendikhan dams, the latter the largest rock-earth filled dam in the world, of 8 million cubic metres of rock. But the local political difficulties intensified, and in 1965 the Baghdad office was closed when the Iraq Government nationalized insurance.

It was in the fifties, and in the years following, that the staff of Toplis and Harding began to travel the world. As one of them remarked, many of the travellers' tales one hears in Toplis and Harding date from this overseas expansion period 'when our London men, in new Horne Bros. safari-suits, were blinking in strong sunlight and trying to communicate in shouted English with the various lesser breeds encountered. . . .'

Some of their experiences could be dramatic. Wyndham 'Binks' Harding found himself in 1956 valuing Methodist missionary stations in Haiti, in the Caribbean. This involved some difficult journeys into the hinterland. One started badly, when one engine of the ancient bomber of the Haitian air force that was to transport him burst into flames as the plane taxied for take-off. What worried Binks Harding more was that the Creole pilot merely paused to extinguish the flames, and then prepared again to take off.

The flight seemed to be progressing reasonably well when there was a bang, and a commotion from the back cabin, where Basil Cawston, an independent surveyor from Jamaica, assisting Toplis and Harding, was sitting with an American tourist who had thumbed a

---

* TOPLIS AND HARDING; International Adjusters MEMORANDUM on Damage to the Installations of IRAQ PETROLEUM COMPANY GROUP in SYRIA, LEBANON, JORDAN and QATAR November – December 1956, 13–14 Union Court, London EC2. Undated: from internal evidence, autumn 1958

lift. Cawston came forward to the flight deck and shouted to Binks Harding, who was sitting beside the pilot, that a door had blown open. The pilot nodded cheerfully and the flight continued.

Heading for a landing at Port-au-Prince, the pilot put the nose down and operated the wheel-lowering gear. At this point all the warning lights flashed and klaxons sounded. Even the pilot seemed slightly perturbed, explaining that he couldn't tell whether the wheels were down, and if they were down, locked. He decided to fly past the control tower.

The flight controller confirmed that the wheels were down, but of course no one could tell whether they were locked. So they prepared for a crash landing. The landing was bumpy, but the wheels held. As the aircraft slowed to a stop, Binks Harding looked back into the cabin and saw the American tourist, ashen-faced, preparing to throw himself out of the open door. Basil Cawston sat bemused, pen and paper on his lap.

'Whatever had you said to him?' asked Binks later.

'Well – as we were coming in to land, I simply asked him if he had a life policy that covered unscheduled flights, and if not, to sign here,' said Basil.

Overseas commissions could take Toplis and Harding staff to extremes of temperature. Not long after the Caribbean experience, Binks Harding found himself examining the results of a plant fire in a construction site on the Greenland ice-cap. He was warned by a local missionary that the Eskimos were so very hospitable and friendly that it could become embarrassing, particularly when they showed honour to distinguished guests by offering their wives for company. It was on his return from that trip that Binks proudly presented his wife with a shoulder-bag made from polar bear fur. It was gratefully received – until, when the weather became warmer, it became clear that the skin had not been properly cured, and the smell was intolerable.

The Toplis and Harding travellers found that the English sense of humour could be misunderstood abroad. During the reconstruction of the main underground system in Hamburg, tunnelling was taking place near an existing station. The walls had slipped, cracking the station roof. Passengers were endangered by falling masonry. Binks Harding went to examine this situation, accompanied by a British engineer and a Lloyd's broker. An inspection of the problem site was followed by a convivial dinner. Next morning, a meeting of some twenty interested parties was convened at the Rathaus. The engineer put forward various possible courses of action: the erection of a false ceiling, cutting out the offending section and grouting, and so on. Meanwhile the broker appeared to have fallen asleep. Binks kicked him under the table. He came to life, and murmured: 'I have the solution. When you issue a ticket, issue each passenger with a steel helmet.'

A period of silence followed, while this was solemnly digested. Then a senior local figure said reprovingly in German: 'Please tell Mr Smith that would be much too expensive.'

It was on one of these trips that Binks Harding (a tall and bulky figure then as now) realized that each meeting would end with a deeply formal exchange of calling cards, even when people had met each other several times before. It seemed that the cards of one German contact got bigger and bigger each time, until some were almost the size of postcards.

He therefore had printed the smallest calling card possible, measuring less than an inch by an inch-and-a-half. At the end of his next meeting with his German contact, he was presented with another huge card. He produced from his breast pocket one of his tiny cards, and put it on the table. The contact looked at it for a moment; and then, very slowly, and for the first time ever, the hint of a smile crept across his face.

It was always Binks Harding's view that while business was serious, it could be eased by humour. He was pleased to find that the serious Japanese appreciated this better than some Europeans. Faced with the famous tiny calling card, one Japanese laughed: 'Ho! Such a small card! Such a big man!'

Another problem resulting from Middle East oil arose soon afterwards in Iran. Until 1951 the substantial oilfields of Iran, most of them in the south-west of the country near Abadan on the Persian Gulf, were operated by the Anglo-Iranian Oil Company under a concession granted by the Shah. In that year, his Prime Minister Mossadeq announced the nationalization of oil production. There followed a period of uncertainty leading to the establishment in 1957 of a consortium of eight oil companies. This consortium, comprising one British, one French, one Dutch and five American companies, was to take over the production, refining and sale of oil, while 'non-basic' operations were the responsibility of the National Iranian Oil Company.

Following the setting up of this consortium, it was necessary to prepare an inventory of the fixed assets of the oilfields. The contract for this job was negotiated by Jock Sutherland. He had become a partner in 1955. A man of considerable personality and unusual history – he had been a film actor and a singer – this was one of his major activities for Toplis and Harding: he left in 1962 to join Graham Miller. To carry out the job, a separate company was formed – Toplis and Harding (Overseas) Ltd, with Alexander Findlay of Toplis and Harding and Findlay as Managing-Director. The survey team, as then mobilized, initially led by Alec Findlay himself, were mostly 'hired guns', that is to say outside specialists and technicians temporarily engaged for the term of the contract (though two young men, Tom Hudson and Tim Bush, were later retained in permanent service to become T. and H. personalities). Another especially important member was the venerable and hugely expert John Strachan, who had recently retired as Chief Plant Inspector, after a working lifetime in Abadan Refinery (and author of the classic *Petroleum Refinery Engineer's Handbook*).

This team of up to twelve people laboured in the Persian Gulf and Oilfields area from October 1960 to Christmas 1961 in arduous conditions of very high Fahrenheit and with due care for local susceptibilities arising from the intensive efforts towards 'Iranianization' that distinguished the period. Subsequently, in London, the field data (often sweatily pencilled under a hot sun) had to be collated and printed into the Inventory, which finally emerged as fifteen massive volumes, of such weight that 100 copies had to be freighted to Iran by sea.

Tom Hudson recalls personally checking some of the assets in what was then the largest oil refinery in the world, including 8000 electric motors and 6000 pumps. Even at the end of the job there were some decisions left uncertain. The inventory was of fixed assets: one of the largest assets at Abadan was a huge floating crane. Surely, some Iranian engineers argued, it could not be included as a 'fixed asset' since it was most assuredly not fixed, but floating.

From time to time there were other misunderstandings. At the very outset, the London office received a telex from Stuart Lynch who had gone to Iran to set up the project, and had early run into the mysterious delaying tactics often encountered in the Middle East. The team would need, he said, lots of soft soap. The London office took this literally. The staff were sent out to buy quantities of soft soap; and at least one member of the staff was despatched to Iran carrying in his luggage a large industrial drum of soft soap. . . . The Toplis and Harding and Findlay team were to be very, very clean.

Other culture shocks met them in the field. Clive Terrill was once crossing the very hot desert south of Naft Safid, trying to follow barely visible wheel-tracks parallel with a pipeline, when the car bogged down immovably in the edge of a sand-dune. With no more than a pint of water, Terrill trekked back for some hours in 120 degrees of Fahrenheit, wild panic and a deteriorating physical condition, often balancing on top of the pipeline itself; until mercifully some indication of company in a very lonely world appeared on the shimmering skyline – a tiny boy with a flock of goats.

Terrill was led by this youth and the goats to a distant herdsmen's compound, and was received at first with blank astonishment but then with the warmest kindness and concern. Watered and rested, he finally feasted with these grave and courteous folk, squatting in a congenial circle under the moon and stars, with no single word of English, Farsi or Arabic that could be exchanged. Nevertheless his hosts made it clear that he was to sleep on a kind of raised pallet, or rough bedstead, in the relative coolness of the open air, while they stretched out on the ground.

This in fact was what led to some little reduction of the general harmony. During the night, Terrill was literally shaken awake by a violent juddering, caused by a large sheep that was massaging itself rapturously against the foot of the 'bedstead'. Stealthily, he drew back a leg and rammed his heel into the flank of the animal – which bolted like a mustang, followed by all of its fellows, jumping and trampling over the supine herdsmen, who leapt to their feet and vanished in furious pursuit of the stampede. Terrill, appalled, and alone in the settling dust, feigned deep and undisturbed sleep; but he remains troubled to this day by the memory of the slight but obvious change in his hosts' manner the following morning.

This hospitable tradition of the desert was universal, though the tribesmen must sometimes have wondered at the ways of their guests. At Izeh, remote in the Zagros mountains, the team visited the winter quarters of the romantic Bakhtiari tribe of nomads, who were then absent on their seasonal wanderings, with the exception of a 'skeleton staff' left in charge. The Headman invited the team to spend the night in his house, and arranged a great feast. One of his tribe was the champion eater of the district, who was reputed to eat a whole lamb at a sitting. Among the contributions made to the feast by the British visitors was a large can of peaches: the champion eater lived up to his reputation by downing the contents in one gulp.

The next morning there were other misfortunes. One of the team determined to demonstrate golf to the chief; but teeing off with great vigour, he managed to drive a quantity of sand and gravel into the headman's face. While he was recovering, amid profuse apologies and explanations, other members of the team were desperately cleaning out the chief's bathing pool. This was an excavated hollow, lined with stone, filled with beautifully clear water, and about five feet across. Some team members had discovered that the butter stored in vacuum jars had melted; they decided to wash the jars out in the pool. Then, to their horror, they saw a thick film of grease spreading across the pool; and while the chief was being persuaded to continue with his golf lesson, other team members were round the back of the house, desperately trying to bail out the butter from his pool.

There were other more serious emergencies in Iran. There was the occasion in Masjid-i-Suleiman when Clive Terrill thought he had summoned a doctor to examine David Russon when he went down with suspected appendicitis. Soon after, a man presented himself at the door, carrying a small black bag. He was led into David Russon's room, but seemed curiously reluctant to examine him. He was persuaded to do so; opening the bag, he produced a tape measure and – to Russon's horror – began to measure him. . . . It was eventually established that he was a rather surprised tailor from the bazaar. A doctor did eventually arrive, and said that Russon must go to hospital. After a long wait, no ambulance arrived, and eventually in desperation Tom Hudson found his way to the local hospital, discovered an ambulance, and persuaded the driver to come to their house. The driver also seemed strangely reluctant, but evidently feeling that he must humour this distressed Englishman, drove him out to the team's house. Tom Hudson thought he had explained that the ambulance was wanted to take a sick man to hospital, and went inside to collect his sick colleague. Returning to the door, he was appalled to see the ambulance disappearing down the street, the driver evidently supposing that his function as a taxi service was completed. . . . Eventually David Russon was taken to hospital, and survived.

In Abadan, where the team were renting a house, they discovered that food was proving to be very expensive; and on looking at the accounts, they found that among other items, Clive Terrill was allegedly consuming 100 kilos of carrots a week. . . . Faced with this, and given the sack on the spot, the butler who was responsible (and who was discovered later to have pocketed some £700 from his frauds) jumped onto his bicycle and rode resentfully off. It was only as his figure was disappearing dustily into the distance that the T and H team remembered that it was not in fact his bicycle. They had bought it to enable him to go down to the market. . . .

In the Middle East, the valuer often had to use his ingenuity. Once, in Bahrain, Tom Hudson was asked to value a dhow. An engineering training had not equipped him with a professional knowledge of dhows. This one, owned by a local sheik, was clearly in the top rank since it had been equipped to carry American tourists: in the middle of the deck was a hut, inside which was a WC (though in use it was virtually impossible to close the door, since there was no knee-room between bowl and door). This amenity, replacing the customary 'thunder-box' overhanging the stern, was thought a strong selling-point. The best way to value it, Hudson suggested (and the sheik agreed) was to test the market by advertising it in the local paper. This was done; and the sheik received such a good offer that he sold the dhow forthwith.

In 1968, with the retirement of Alec Findlay, Toplis and Harding and Findlay became Toplis and Harding and Partners.

9. Hurricane

THE LATER fifties and early sixties were a period of consolidation. Two new partners were introduced in 1955: James Sutherland and F. G. Geddes. 'Freddie' Geddes had run his own company (Geddes Johnston); he specifically liked accident work, and also dealt with the major jewellery cases. He also built up a considerable reputation in the film industry: for example, he dealt with the multi-million-pound claim when the film *Cleopatra* was delayed by the illness of Elizabeth Taylor. He was a chain-smoker, and seemed to have only one suit, which was perpetually grey with cigarette ash and known around the office as his 'Players suit'.

Elizabeth Taylor as Cleopatra.

In Paris, Ian Campbell had joined his father Arthur Campbell (who had returned to reopen the office in 1945, after helping to keep the London office in business throughout the war). Ian Campbell, while working in Paris, was appointed to the London partnership in 1956; father and son were partners together for two years, until Arthur Campbell's retirement in 1958.

In May 1959 there was a profound shock when Dudley Strevens, son-in-law of Stanley Leftwich and much liked and respected in the office and throughout the profession, took his own life. It was the more distressing because it was totally unexpected and unpredicted. One of his many services to the firm was that he recruited Robert Cole, who was made a partner in 1960.

Ninian Hawken retired from the partnership at the end of September 1961, mainly because of ill-health. He had lost a lung during the war, and found breathing difficult. He was persuaded to maintain his links with the Toplis and Harding office as a consultant, a presence warmly welcomed by the insurance market. He died at his home near Chelmsford in July 1975. James Perry and F. J. Gould retired at the end of that year. Perry had in 1941 helped to found the Association of Fire Loss Adjusters, and was its Honorary Secretary until 1951–2 when he was elected Deputy President and then President. It was typical of him that after his year in office, he unpretentiously reverted to being Honorary Secretary again. In 1961 the Association became the Chartered Institute of Loss Adjusters; in 1965 he was presented with a silver salver and cheque in recognition of his 25 years' service. Freddie Gould was a less public figure; but the partners had reason to appreciate his quiet efficiency, particularly in picking up the pieces and getting business started again after the office was blitzed.

As if the elements needed to mark Ninian Hawken's retirement with high drama, on the night of 30 October 1961 Hurricane 'Hattie' struck the coast of Central America, devastating much of the colony of British Honduras. Winds of up to 200 miles an hour swept four or five feet of sea water inland, producing such unusual effects as dead fish in upstairs wardrobes and in locked cars. The precise wind speed was never fixed locally, because the wind gauge at the local airport snapped off at 180 mph. A blanket of black mud covered everything. Most houses were of wood, and built on stilts as a precaution against flooding; some now leant at crazy angles, and others had been blown away altogether.

Donald Buckham and Philip Ottaway flew in from London to supervise the checking of claims. They were joined by William Brown, who happened to be 'minding the store' in Trinidad for six months while the local manager was on leave, and by Ted Hill – manager of the Jamaica office – who did the book-keeping. At first there was no hotel accommodation, no running water or electricity, and no office equipment or stationery. A company of British troops had been flown in from Jamaica to join the small local garrison; a British frigate hove to opposite the capital, Belize, and the ship's company helped with the clearance work.

The Toplis and Harding team began assessing claims shortly before Christmas. It was a difficult and tedious business; the team had to tour the country in Army vehicles, often finding nothing left but the piles on which a property once stood. From the remaining layout the adjusters would measure the probable square area, and apply a multiplier guided by a local quantity surveyor familiar with local building materials. The damage was visible everywhere. The forests that had provided Europe with a great deal of its mahogany through-out the nineteenth century were cut with swathes of devastation, and some of the tops of the tall pines round Stann Creek were twisted off, as if by some huge extra-terrestrial hand.

But, despite all this, work went on. At the new year Donald Buckham was made a junior partner, and to mark this Wyndham Harding sent out a crate of Gordon's gin and another of Johnny Walker whisky, both much appreciated. They would perhaps have been even more appreciated if the team had not already succeeded in accumulating quantities of liquid salvage of a similar kind during their persistent enquiries. Since the humidity of British Honduras is perpetually around 97 per cent, cool drinks are an essential support.

Eventually 4000 claims were handled by the team on the London market. It was said that through the Toplis and Harding team insur-ers put more money into the local economy than had ever before gone through the local banks. For their part, the people of British Honduras began once again to live more normal lives. Though a small British garrison has continued to patrol the contested border with Guatemala, a new capital was completed inland. The country was renamed Belize (the name of the old capital) in 1973, and achieved independence in 1981.

It was experiences of this sort about which Donald Buckham spoke when he gave a paper before the Insurance Institute of London on 25 February 1963. By this time he was much experienced, having run the Toplis and Harding offices in India and in Australia. His account (see Appendix I) well reflects his humour and commonsense, which were to serve Toplis and Harding for many more years, until his much regretted death in 1989.

10. Paris, Europe and the World

THE PARIS office had been in the hands of Arthur Campbell between the wars. It was he who took into the French office in Rue Richelieu a youngster, straight from school, whose parents were living in Paris: Durban Squire. In those days the French partnership had no formal links with the London partnership of Toplis and Harding, other than that Graham Harding was a partner in both (and, in effect, the modern founder of both). It became a Société Anonyme (S.A.) in 1919. Business increased. There were three executive members of the Board, Arthur Campbell (known as Administrateur Délégué) with Charles Vanson and George Champion. Other adjusters (known in those days as 'assessors') were Jack Soanes, a relative of Arthur Campbell who was later to manage the Antwerp office, and Frank W. Ford, who appropriately specialized in motor claims and also dealt with many losses under a Lloyd's policy covering the third-party liability of a firm of bomb disposal specialists, Pickett & Sons, in connection with injuries to cattle and other property during the destruction of ammunition and unexploded bombs and mines in northern France in the years following the First World War. Another adjuster was a young Frenchman, M. Bourdelot, who tried hard to perfect his colloquial English; but it deserted him – when infuriated by one English colleague he would cry: 'You get on my nose!' Finally there was Albert Angelo Gregory, who specialized in jewellery and fine art. He had a great sense of humour, and was a dapper, white-haired man of considerable style, smoking his cigarettes through a long holder. He used to put on a fine act for wealthy ladies who were distressed at finding their jewellery stolen, as they believed. 'My dear Duchess,' he would purr, 'please don't worry any more about your loss. Leave the whole thing to me. There is no need to concern yourself. . . .' And having comforted the lady he would withdraw, shut the door, turn to the young colleague accompanying him, and mutter: 'Stupid old bitch, she's just mislaid the stuff somewhere. . . .'

The office manager through much of the twenties was Miss Margaret Reid, who had arrived to be Arthur Campbell's secretary but who, when promoted, proved to be not only extremely efficient but also a stern disciplinarian to all the staff, the results of which enhanced the reputation of the firm still further.

In 1922 a subsidiary office was opened in Strasbourg (to cope with German business) managed by A. J. C. Eveleigh, and shortly afterwards others in Milan and Genoa, managed by Wilfred Brinkman; but after the accession of Mussolini to power, in 1932, the office for Italian business was moved to Nice (that office was also well placed to serve the large and rich expatriate British community in that town). In 1925 Toplis and Harding S.A. was awarded the Lloyd's agency in Paris. The Paris office continued to be profitable until the outbreak of the Second World War.

Most of these offices were able (being French-registered) to continue operations until the fall of France in June 1940. The Paris office formally closed on 12 June 1940. Arthur Campbell and his wife Valentine escaped from Paris at the last moment through Bordeaux. They arrived by air at Croydon at the height of a German bombing raid on the London docks, and were not pleased to be shown, while waiting for the end of the raid, into a room with a domed glass roof. Matters went rather worse for A. J. C. Eveleigh, the manager of the Strasbourg branch; English-born, but a fluent French and German speaker, he was arrested (with his son) and consigned to the St Denis detention camp. So, by chance, was Wilfred Brinkman, the manager of the Nice office. Brinkman was a resentful and uncooperative prisoner and the occupying forces moved him to a concentration camp in Germany. However, he survived and returned to Paris in 1945 (with, it is said, a beard down to his waist) and it was Wilfred Brinkman who reopened the Paris office.

The office had been kept ticking over during the war by two devoted secretaries, Mlle. Jeanne Garnier and Mlle. Odette Pasquier (the latter to become, some years later, Mrs Durban Squire). Legally it was run by an administrator appointed by the French authorities on behalf of the German occupying power: the administrator was a M. Durand, who had been the representative in Paris of the Southern Railway.

After the war Arthur Campbell (having spent the war years as a mainstay of the London office) returned to Paris, and was joined on his demobilization from the army by his son Ian. In the late 1950s, Lloyd's underwriters led by Cuthbert Heath and others asked two firms of adjusters, one of them Toplis and Harding, to open an office in Switzerland. Durban Squire became manager of Adjusters (Switzerland) Ltd. The Strasbourg and Nice offices were also reopened, but on Eveleigh's retirement Strasbourg closed, followed in 1977 by Nice (whose manager, Jean-Jacques Audidier, later worked for their successors). In the years after 1945, the largest piece of business dealt with by the Paris office was in relation to the Insurance Company of North America, which insured the cars and property of US Army officers in Europe (since Lloyd's had not then returned to Europe). This business was then superseded by similar work for the USAA (United Services Automobile Association) of San Antonio, Texas, whose commissions provided about half the business of the office, marine and non-marine. When General De Gaulle determined to expel American forces from France in 1966, this business ended almost overnight, and it was fortunate for Toplis and Harding that at just this time Lloyd's began to return to the French market, following the French Warranty Co.

Ian Campbell, having taken over from his father, husbanded the business throughout a difficult post-war period and into calmer waters. During all this time he was Président Directeur Général and, as director of the Lloyd's and Institute of London Underwriters agencies, responsible to them for the performance not only of his own agency but also for his sub-agents. He was succeeded in 1989 by Philip Ottaway, but remains as a Consultant – 40 years of uninterrupted service.

The Toplis and Harding office in Antwerp was closed in 1961 (though there was subsequently a brief association in that city with Kiewits – there was a longer association in Holland). There were other retrenchments and reorganizations in those years: the Teheran office was closed (because of the difficulties of business in the political climate that was to lead two years later to the Iranian revolution and the expulsion of the Shah), as was the Toplis and Harding office in Bombay – Donald Buckham, who had been running it, moved to Australia to run the Toplis and Harding offices in Perth and Melbourne. Following the Suez affair, and Farrell's retirement to the UK, the long-standing formal association in the Middle East with Farrell, Ajus and Ghazarian of Cairo and Cyprus also ended. Toplis and Harding (Middle East) was set up at the instigation of the British Government to deal with desequestration of British property.

With the retirement of Ninian Hawken, J. W. Perry and F. J. Gould at the end of 1961, Wyndham Harding, Freddie Geddes, Robert Cole and Ian Campbell (the last now back in Paris) remained as partners. The London office was still comparatively small, with 25 professional staff and a consolidated net fee income of around £100,000. Nevertheless the reputation of Toplis and Harding at Lloyd's, upheld with such distinction by Ninian Hawken in the post-war years, was maintained by his cousin Wyndham 'Binks' Harding. Tall, bulky, warmhearted, thoroughly gregarious, he was welcomed by many older brokers who remembered his distinguished father Graham Harding with respect and affection, and found that many of his attributes were continued in his son. 'Binks' was thoroughly a Lloyd's man, and to walk with him round the market was to observe the friendliness with which he was received.

In the early sixties Ninian Hawken's retirement was followed by a couple of years of rethinking in the London office. In 1964 Freddie Geddes joined from Geddes Johnston. Dennis Tieman joined the partnership in January 1963, initially to look after contract claims; he was to serve it well, latterly in charge of the fire department until he retired. Many regarded him as one of the most skilled loss adjusters of his time.

Before the Second World War the London partnership of Toplis and Harding consisted of two distinct parts, one concerned with loss adjusting and the other maintaining the older traditional function of auctioneering and valuation. While Graham Harding was a partner in both sides of the business, Humphrey Russell ran the auctioneering activities between the wars. On his death during the war, this function of the firm was virtually suspended. It was, however, reactivated in 1958, as Toplis and Harding and Findlay, with Alexander Findlay and Clive Terrill as the founding partners, and with James Perry representing the parent Toplis and Harding. This was the first of the 'technical' satellites (evolving later into Toplis and Harding and Partners, Toplis and Harding Technical, etc.) concerned, initially, with value-at-risk assessment, risk-surveys, and supporting T and H adjusters with consultancy in building and plant machinery losses.

Sometimes this could lead to startling experiences. On one occasion Clive Terrill went to investigate some damage to chimney stacks at the London Brick Company, on whose Stewartby site the tall chimneys throng the fields like the tall pillars of some industrial temple. The weather was terrible, with strong winds and rain. Arriving on site, Clive Terrill could see no-one to ask; so, to save time, he climbed up a chimney, clinging firmly on as the wind blew more fiercely. He inspected the damage and descended to the ground, shaken but safe. Eventually he found a steeplejack in a nearby hut. He, asked to confirm Terrill's findings, said firmly: 'I wouldn't think of climbing in weather like this!'

Among the notable cases with which Toplis and Harding was involved at this time was the loss adjusting following what became popularly known as the Great Train Robbery, when in the early morning of Thursday 8 August 1963, a gang stopped and robbed a mail train near Leatherslade Farm in Buckinghamshire. The haul consisted of more than half a million pounds (then a huge sum) in used bank notes being returned to the major clearing banks in London. At least one of the banks proved to be uninsured, but the number of claims that followed the crime was considerable; several of the major London adjusters were involved, Toplis and Harding among them.

Another historic phase ended in 1964, with the liquidation of Toplis and Harding (Northern) Ltd. This firm, founded in the 1920s by Graham Harding, had its own curious corner of history since at least one meeting of the partnership was held in the Gentlemen's lavatory at Piccadilly station, Manchester, with the (lady) company secretary posted outside – it was the only convenient place between the arrival of the London train and the departure of the train to Chester, where Harding and various important clients were having a working day at the races.

On Graham Harding's death in 1949 his son agreed to sell his 50 per cent holding in Toplis and Harding (Northern) Ltd to the London partnership. This arrangement continued for 15 years until William Burkinshaw, the Manchester partner and chief executive of Toplis and Harding (Northern) Limited, announced his wish to retire. Unfortunately there seemed to be very little on paper about the precise legal and financial arrangements for the partnership (Graham Harding had belonged firmly to the generation of 'gentlemen's agreements' on a handshake: while this was adequate during his lifetime, it made difficulties for his successors). Eventually, though not without some unhappiness, Toplis and Harding (Northern) Limited was liquidated and the business became the Manchester office of the London partnership.

At about that time also Toplis and Harding became involved in events that were to lead to the purchase of the long-established Dublin firm of Walter Hume & Co. Walter Hume was a Scot, born in Edinburgh and trained as an assessor with Cruickshank & Co. in that city. In 1888 he was encouraged by the Northern Insurance Co. to open an office in Dublin, and this he did with the approval of John Cruickshank who wrote of him that 'he possesses a good sound judgement, is firm and courteous in his manner, attentive and painstaking, and thoroughly conscientious in his decisions'. His first report concerned fire damage in Londonderry, and was for the Sun Insurance Office (an interesting augury, perhaps, for his firm's future association with Toplis and Harding, whose founder had worked for that distinguished office).

He built his company into one of high reputation. On Hume's death in 1921 he was succeeded by his son, John Hume, with other partners. On the deaths of those partners in 1953, Hume was approached by Graham Miller & Co. of London to form an association. During the negotiations, Graham Miller recruited yet another bright young Scot, J. H. Smith, then with the Edinburgh firm of McLaren Dick & Co., to join Walter Hume & Co. in Dublin. He had been (in 1949) the first student to join the Association of Fire Loss Adjusters (as it then was) by examination.

As it happened, the negotiations between Walter Hume & Co. and Graham Miller broke down. But James H. 'Jimmy' Smith remained in Dublin; and having become a Fellow of the Chartered Institute of Loss Adjusters in 1958, he purchased the sole partnership of Walter Hume & Co. in 1963. In 1964 Toplis and Harding purchased first a 51 per cent share, and in 1966 the remaining 49 per cent, and the Belfast office became a branch of Toplis and Harding. In 1967 Toplis and Harding purchased from Smith the goodwill of Walter Hume & Co., which thereafter became in effect the Dublin branch of Toplis and Harding, while retaining the old name, and J. H. Smith as manager, with a partnership in the London firm.

Amid these developments, the London office was again moving home; at the end of 1964 the lease of 13/14 Union Court, off Old Broad Street, was given up, and the office moved to the upper floors of 16 Park House, Finsbury Circus. In 1965 a substantial amount of work was brought in by Hurricane Betsy, which did considerable damage in the Bahamas. The accounts for that year also revealed a historical curiosity. The firm's bankers, Coutts & Co., had on deposit the sum of £7327 'which represents the accumulation of capital and interest on the agents' fees payable in respect of a successfully concluded claim which arose prior to 1939 [concerning a fire in the part of Galatz] and was settled post 1945, the fee being held in trust as the agent is resident in an East European country'. The agent was, in fact, resident in Romania; and, possibly due to the thaw in the cold war, arrangements were evidently made for him to be paid the fee.

The next considerable expansion took place in 1967. In February that year, at the request of the local insurance market, a branch office was opened in Sheffield (by William Brown): it was at first mainly to service the Sun Alliance Insurance and the Halifax Building Society. A branch was opened in Bristol in October. With the acquisition of Belfast and Dublin, this much widened Toplis and Harding's provincial representation. This was to be yet further increased in the next two years with the opening of branches in Glasgow, Newcastle and Reading.

In 1967, largely on the initiative of Wyndham Harding, the scope of the partnership's services was also widened by the creation of Toplis and Harding Marine in the business of marine cargo surveyors. These were the years when 'containerization' was being introduced, and therefore the techniques of cargo surveying were changing in tune with these innovations. Toplis and Harding was fortunate to recruit W. E. 'Bill' Astle to head what was initially a department. Astle had been Deputy Controller of Agencies at Lloyd's, and therefore had great expertise in the marine insurance market. He was assisted in setting up the new department by a master mariner, R. F. Jones.

The department steadily increased its business not only in the marine insurance market but also in the protection and indemnity market covered by the P. and I. Clubs. To strengthen the staff in the administrative areas, in 1969 Donald Johnston joined, having for many years been in the business of marine insurance and surveying, and recently retired from managing an important Lloyd's Agency. As some of the P. and I. Associations were developing new schemes of special coverage for those concerned with the transport of goods in containers, the marine department began to specialize in this area. The number of thefts from containers, and thefts of complete container loads, was growing, and the expertise of Toplis and Harding Marine in the resolution of claims in this area became recognized.

At the same time the business of general cargo surveying was also growing. A notable case concerned a major oil company constructing an oil terminal in the Middle East. Component parts manufactured in various factories in Britain and in Germany were arriving damaged, and needed to be replaced. This led to heavy insurance claims, and also delays in completion. When another terminal was to be built, the marine department was commissioned to survey the transit of parts. This involved visiting the manufacturer to oversee the loading of parts for transit to the ports, where one of the master mariner surveyors would superintend the loading (particularly important for the stowing of the terminal's loading arms, which could be damaged if put beneath heavy cargo). The service was successful, and on this occasion all the parts arrived undamaged. The oil company thereafter used Toplis and Harding for similar work.

These developments proved so successful that from 1971 a separate partnership of Toplis and Harding Marine was created within the framework of the main partnership, with offices at Barking, Essex.

Following this, offices were opened outside London, Dublin in 1971, Manchester in 1972, and Belfast in 1980. In 1987 an office was opened in Ipswich to take advantage of the increasing traffic passing through the ports of Felixstowe and Harwich.

The first Toplis and Harding office in the Middle East, in Cairo, was closed in 1956 following the Suez fiasco, when the second (Baghdad) office was started, only to close again when the Khassem regime came to power in Iraq. However, in 1967 it was decided to enlarge the partnership's interests in the Middle East. This had previously been overseen by Ninian Hawken. But then an international company was set up in the Channel Islands, of which Beirut was the first branch. The enterprise was jointly set up with Terence Mulford of Mulford & Co., the correspondent of Toplis in the Middle East (Mulford's son Christopher was at this time finding increasing work in Saudi Arabia: however, he was wanted to assist in his father's business). The branch was set up with a capital of 7500 Lebanese lire (£750), and the first year's premium by Toplis and Harding for the life policy of its new representative to be based in Beirut – Roger Schwab.

Schwab arrived in Lebanon on 27 May 1967 and was met at Beirut Airport by Ninian Hawken with Terence Mulford, who told him that the climate was deteriorating. Indeed it was. The relations between Israel and the Arab states were escalating towards military conflict. President Nasser of Egypt had made a pact with King Hussein of Jordan, and had required the United Nations peace-keeping force to withdraw from the Gaza strip. Israel saw this as a prelude to another Arab attack, and on Monday 5 June the Israeli air force made pre-emptive strikes against 19 air bases of the United Arab Republics. Within days Israeli troops moved to take the Sinai peninsula, the Gaza strip, and the West Bank of the Jordan.

Hostilities ended on 10 June, from which the incident became known as the 'Six Days' War'. It left Israel in effective control of large areas of additional territory, and with responsibility for 750,000 Palestinian Arabs on the West Bank, and a further 300,000 in the Gaza strip – the source of increasing trouble in the years that followed.

During the Six Days' War, and for several days before and after, Roger Schwab was marooned with the rest of the British community in Beirut's Excelsior Hotel. This was no great problem, since apart from one air raid in the early days of the conflict, there was little military activity in Beirut. However, the war brought to the surface the simmering rivalries between the various sections of the Beirut population (of which about 50 per cent were Christian and 34 per cent Muslim); and as the Israelis took over territories that were previously Muslim, there was increasing bitterness against the British and Americans in Beirut, and damage arose to their property. It was the first round in a devastating conflict that was to destroy a once beautiful and prosperous city.

Later that year there were riots in southern Arabia, in Aden. The former British colony had become partially self-governing in 1962; in the following year it was incorporated into the Federation of South Arabia. However, there was continuing and growing civil unrest, stirred up by revolutionary groups as the British forces prepared to leave.

The last days of the British presence in Aden were policed by a British military force from the Argyll and Sutherland Highlanders, commanded by Lieut-Col. Colin Mitchell – soon familiarly known to the British public as 'Mad Mitch' for the vigour and speed with which he directed retribution on the riotous trouble-makers (he was later to be Member of Parliament for West Aberdeenshire). But 'Mad Mitch' and his staff had admirably accurate knowledge of where incidents had happened; and so Roger Schwab, who had been joined by Robert Cole, found himself touring the trouble-spots in Aden each morning with an armed escort, inspecting the riot's damaged (and sometimes undamaged) properties with the gun barrel from the turret of a Saracen armoured car waving over their heads, while soldiers flushed out the buildings.

Seldom can adjusters have had more professional assistance in identifying the precise state of property. They were well able to rule on the accuracy or otherwise of claims from property owners (many of whom had judiciously left the territory before the troubles started – and some of whom had forgotten, by some oversight, that before leaving they had sold the properties on which they were now claiming).

During Roger Schwab's ten years in Beirut, the great expansion of commercial activity in the Middle East, fuelled by oil wealth, led to the opening of Toplis and Harding branches in Kuwait, Dubai, Oman, and briefly once again (1975–6) in Teheran. An off-shore branch was also opened in Cyprus, though its effectiveness was somewhat reduced by the earlier Turkish invasion and subsequent partition of the island between Greek and Turkish Cypriots. This office, however, was the springboard for the Jeddah, Riyadh and Al Khobar offices in Saudi Arabia, started in 1983.

Other 'incidents' on which Roger Schwab was invited to report took him to Casablanca, where a senior official of a bank had absconded with quantities of cash. In the course of the visit, Schwab called on the local chief of police who, delighted to be consulted, insisted on providing a tour of inspection of the facilities of his police station. These included a comprehensively-equipped torture chamber (not, at that moment, in use; although it seemed that the enthusiastic police chief would willingly have arranged a demonstration if requested).

On another occasion, in Saudi Arabia, Schwab found himself spending a night in a police cell – fortunately as an honoured guest. His car had crashed in the desert; since unfortunately the occupant of the car into which his driver had crashed happened to be the local sheik, the driver was promptly arrested, leaving Schwab in the desert. Seeing a distant light, he made for it, and found that it was a police post, with an 'arresting' police sergeant eager to provide him with a bed for the night. The light was courteously left on, enabling him to spend several hours watching a large beetle climbing up the wall and across the ceiling, until it fell, with dreadful regularity, onto his prostrate form.

In Kabul, to investigate a fire in the roof of the new nightclub of an international hotel (probably started deliberately either by local people disapproving of this innovation, or by disaffected staff), living conditions were naturally somewhat more comfortable. (These were not good conditions for writing reports: Roger Schwab reckons that to write a report, one should book into the worst available hotel, preferably on or near an airport, and swear not to leave it until the report is completed.) There was also some sport: the British community in Kabul were playing the Russians at football – and then discovered that the middle-aged but agile Russian centre-forward was a former Olympic team member, the Stanley Matthews of Novosibirsk. The manager of the local Marks & Spencer store happened to be a former cricketing friend of Schwab's. The Kabul store, at least in those days, had a neon sign announcing 'Marks & Sparks'. Local shareholders had arranged it whilst the manager was on leave, hearing the company so referred to, and assuming it was the correct name. A London representative of the company, discovering that business had increased since the sign had been put up, allowed it to remain, probably the only such sign which ever existed in the history of that distinguished store.

But if Kabul had its social pleasures, Schwab was not allowed to enjoy them for long. Having completed his report and cabled it to London, he was indulging himself with a swim in the hotel pool when he was called out to take a telephone call. It was Ninian Hawken, from London. 'Roger – now that you've finished, could you

The Toplis and Harding office in Arthur Street (from a line and wash drawing by David Fletcher).

96

stop off in Teheran on your way back? I'd like you to take a look at another problem. . . .' It was an example of the long arm of Toplis and Harding. At the end of his decade in Beirut Roger Schwab returned to London in 1978 and became a Toplis and Harding partner.

By 1970 the fee income of Toplis and Harding had trebled in a decade to over £300,000, with net profit increased in proportion. The London office moved to Arthur Street. The partners at this time were Wyndham Harding, Robert Cole, Donald Buckham, John B. Evans, F. Wilson Kennedy, Ian Campbell, James E. Smith, J. H. Smith and Quentin G. Seaton; they were joined in 1973 by Donald Johnston, C. F. G. Terrill and William G. Brown. John Evans retired at the end of 1973. In that year new branch offices were opened in Cardiff (run by Huw Rodge), Inverness, Birmingham (run by William Brown), Carmarthen and Enfield.

In Europe, the Fribourg office (originally a joint venture between Toplis and Harding and Tyler and Co. in the fifties) rejoined the group. Toplis and Harding KG was founded in the Federal Republic of Germany, jointly with Carl Gielisch, a prominent firm of Rhine marine surveyors. In the Middle East, a second Toplis and Harding office was opened, in Kuwait. In Africa, an office was opened in Lusaka, Zambia (by Jim Grant, formerly of Birmingham). In the Far East, an office was opened in Hong Kong (by Austen Parker, who was subsequently to move to Singapore).

11. Earthquake and Cyclone

THERE ARE occasions when the loss adjuster finds himself truly in the wake of disaster. Natural catastrophes happen from time to time; and it is these that are most feared, and against which the prudent citizen insures. Getting to the site of a disaster is often difficult; finding somewhere to stay and to work while making the necessary enquiries may be hazardous.

Beyond that, the victims of natural disasters are often suffering from shock. The two case histories that follow concern a major earthquake in South America, and cyclone damage in Northern Australia. They illustrate some of the problems faced by the Toplis and Harding teams 'on the ground'; and they show also that the loss adjuster pitchforked into such conditions of anarchy has to keep a cool head – and even, despite the very real horrors and problems – a sense of humour.

MANAGUA

Shortly after midnight on 23 December 1972 the market-women of the Nicaraguan capital, Managua, were busily preparing for the final rush of Christmas shoppers. They had not been deterred by two earth tremors, one an hour and the other half an hour earlier. Their city was often shaken by earth tremors; the local people were used to them. But then at 0029 hours there was a major earthquake. The market buildings, together with most other buildings within an area of 5 square kilometres (some 500 blocks on a rectilinear grid), were severely damaged. The vibration of the earthquake, together with falling debris, overturned many charcoal stoves and led to fires that added to the devastation. The fires could not be controlled because the central fire-station was within the zone of worst damage, and some volunteer firemen – arriving on call to fight fires started as a result of the earlier tremors – were killed, and their fire-engines crushed beneath the rubble. The water supply, in any case, was disrupted. In the days that followed there were further losses from fire and substantial looting or pillage.

Looters in the market area of Managua following the earthquake. One girl evidently has clear priorities – she has chosen lengths of dress fabrics.

The land on which the capital of Nicaragua stands is crossed by three known 'fault lines' in the geological stratum that is the 'Pacific Plate'. This extends along the whole western coast of South and North America up to the longitude of Japan. Geologists determined in the mid-sixties that the Pacific Plate is moving northwards at an average of 2.5 ins. per year, and that sudden irregularities in the rate of 'slip' between plate boundaries cause the tectonic type of earthquake. It is along these boundaries or 'fault lines' that earthquakes occur, the most familiarly known being the San Andreas fault associated with the San Francisco earthquake of 1906. The people of Managua were certainly not ignorant of the consequences of earthquakes, since the city had been devastated by one in 1931, and a lesser but serious tremor had hit the city as recently as 1968.

The earthquake that struck Managua early on the morning of 23 December lasted for seven seconds and measured between 6.25 and 6.4 on the Richter Scale. Tremors continued for a total of 43 seconds. Many other earthquakes of varying intensity have been experienced along this coast, and as a result of them there have been changes in building methods. In particular, the wealth of the West Coast of the United States, and the incidence there of much high-rise building, led to legal requirements for property owners to install measuring equipment to monitor earth tremors and their impact on buildings. These monitors provided much information during and after the San Francisco earthquake of 1971 (as they were to again in 1989), which led to moves towards more effective civil engineering and building codes.

The circumstances in Managua were not wholly comparable, since the ground on which the city is built is mainly of volcanic debris and alluvium, with a high water-table (being on the shore of Lake Managua), and is therefore more liable to earthquake damage than other places built on solid rock. In particular, the characteristics of building damage in Managua, and specifically the way in which many concrete-framed buildings collapsed downwards into the ground floor, suggested that there should be more research into the incidence of vertical damage in such circumstances.

Naturally the events following the earthquake were confused and chaotic. The largest fire, starting in the Central Market and soon spreading to a neighbouring 'Mercado San Miguel' could not be contained, because the local survivors were in a state of deep shock, and because the fire station had been demolished in the first moments. The Senior Officer survived, and went immediately to summon assistance from Jinotepe, 29 miles away, where he was able to telephone other

Nicaraguan colleagues. It was well over three hours before the first fire-fighting appliances arrived and started to contain the blaze. They were joined later by appliances from four more distant towns and, later in the day, from Costa Rica. The task was of course complicated by the disruption of water supplies, so that water had to be pumped from Lake Managua.

It seems that the main fires were contained by late on Christmas Eve (though this had not been easy; one building four blocks east of the market was a store for Christmas fireworks and provided a dramatic pyrotechnic display when fire reached it). Once the fire seemed to be contained, the brigade from Costa Rica was stood down and returned home. Unfortunately fires continued to break out through Christmas Day, and in the days thereafter until 31 December. Some at least of these fires were not accidental. 'The events subsequent to December 24 are, to say the least, somewhat obscure,' commented the Toplis and Harding report.

The adjustment of claims in such devastating circumstances can never be a precise science. It does, however, require as much skill, sifting of evidence and persistence as any criminal investigation. Insurance and reinsurance are concerned with the assessment of risk, but there were in this instance additional risks to the insurers that are not always present. The Toplis & Harding representatives were aware of a report in *The Policyholder* following the previous Managua earthquake of 1931, which gave the information that:

> By a recent decree the President of Nicaragua has been authorised to take steps to bring about payment of insurance claims arising out of the fire which broke out in Managua immediately following the earthquake of 31 March 1931. The decree also authorises the President to discontinue the business of any insurance company in Nicaragua which does not abide by the decisions of the local judicial authorities.

Robert Cole, who led the three-strong Toplis and Harding team on this occasion, supported by ten adjusters seconded from other firms (Henry C. Hudson & Co. and Moller & Co.) and an adjuster from Guatemala (Ernesto Zacharisson), was to remark that such a claims situation demands two factors: field work and anticipation.

The consequent claims were mainly within four areas. These were claims relating to direct earthquake damage, to fires resulting from the earthquake, to other fires, and to loss by looting. It was therefore necessary for the team to establish the precise sequence of events, as far as practicable in such a devastating situation. The team set out to find as much visual evidence as possible. Many press photographs were taken of the fires that followed the earthquake and, as these were clearly dated and often identified by time, they provided corroborative evidence. Aerial photographs had been taken on 28 December and again (on 30 December) by the Nicaraguan Air Force: the latter confirmed the continuing spread of fires on that date. The aerial photographs provided a huge jigsaw or mosaic map of Managua. In the Toplis and Harding office in Arthur Street, Tom Hudson gradually assembled the separate shots into a series of coherent maps, taken on different days. But he began to realize that each 'map' had one piece of the jigsaw missing. In each case it was at the same central point in the city. A check with the street map of Managua provided the solution. In the area of the missing shot was the Presidential Palace. In Nicaragua a prudent cameraman does not take pictures of the Presidential Palace from the air.

There was some suspicion, which turned to certainty, that some property-owners set fire to their own premises if they were covered for fire risks but not for (more expensive) earthquake damage. Within a short time the team had established that five factors contributed substantially to the spread of fires. First, though the Managua Fire Brigade had worked well and with determination to contain the fire in its early stages, its members were volunteers, there were no arrangements for men to be relieved or to be fed and quartered, and it was inevitable that sooner or later many firemen went home to look after their own families and secure their own property.

Secondly, it seemed that by Christmas Eve, with the main fire apparently contained, a false sense of security developed (at which time the fire brigade from Costa Rica started for home, only to be recalled three days later). Third, the scale of the disaster impelled the survivors to concentrate on coping with their own personal losses and distresses, leaving no energy or interest to help their neighbours. Fourth, it is possible that some looters started fires either accidentally, or to hide the evidence of their activities (and some looting certainly happened when people from other parts of the city who went to the devastated area out of curiosity observed shopkeepers legitimately removing property from damaged premises; the rubber-neckers, assuming that there was a free-for-all, began looting). Finally, much of the property to the west of the Central Market was of 'taquesal construction', which consists of laths on a timber-frame with mud infilling; as the prevailing wind was a strong easterly, any spark would fan embers and the dry exposed timbers from which the mud (adobe) had collapsed were exposed and readily consumed with renewed fires.

So the main task of the team of adjusters in the days that followed was to establish precisely what happened when, and to what. There was an obvious tendency for property-owners who had not taken out expensive insurance against earthquakes, but had insured against fire, to claim that the damage to their premises was exclusively caused by fire.

It was necessary to create a 'fire plan'. This showed the development of fires in the 500 blocks of the central area of Managua in the days immediately following the earthquake. The excellent aerial photographs taken by the Nicaraguan Air Force were a primary contributor to this, since they clearly showed the smoke billowing from the fire area on the morning of 23 December, and the precise state of devastation on 30 December. The adjusters set out to collect as many as possible of the large number of press photographs taken between those dates. They also took particular note of the statements made by property-owners who had been insured against earthquake, since they were obviously covered and had no reason to falsify evidence. Other property-owners who had been less prescient, and had insured against fire only, were of course eager to argue that their premises had been destroyed by fire; indeed, it seemed sometimes that they were asserting that there had been no earthquake in Managua at all. The Toplis and Harding team had to assemble this immense quantity of paper and photographs in the limited space afforded within the private houses in which they were billeted. The meals were often delayed while one meticulous adjuster removed his papers from the dining-room table in a precise and essential (to him) slow order.

He could not be blamed, for the sequence of events was vital to the 'fire plan', since payments under reinsurance contracts were linked to 24-hour time periods. The 'fire plan' was therefore drawn to show the areas subject to fire in three time-packages: 23–25 December, 26–28 December, and 29–31 December. This could not, of course, allow for every eventuality. Fires may well have caused the eventual collapse of buildings already a structural total loss as a result of the earthquake. Decisions could not, therefore, be made with absolute certainty. But the 'fire plan' provided enough positive evidence to deter those claimants who were inclined to be aggressively imaginative, since it encapsulated on one large sheet of paper all the available hard evidence, and so demonstrated the likelihood or impossibility of some scenarios proffered by those keen to capitalize financially on the disaster.

The looting that went on in the days following the earthquake faced the adjusters with yet another puzzle, this time concerning local law and language, compounded by problems of translation. The Spanish expression for looting is 'pillaje'. The first looting seems to have taken place on the morning after the earthquake, when sight-seers came across property lying on the ground outside damaged or demolished buildings, and simply appropriated it, as 'salvage'.

The sheer volume of the operation is illustrated by the fact that the report records that 280 claims under fire and earthquake policies had been adjusted and settlement effected, and 850 properties insured under housing loan policies had been inspected and the claims adjusted, all within three months of the catastrophic event. Despite the contentious aspects of claims under 'Fire only' policies because of the difficulty of establishing the precise sequence of events (earthquake, consequent fire, subsequent fire, and later damage through looting or malice), settlements were ultimately arrived at amounting to approximately 25 per cent of the sums insured exposed, those sums totalling about $20 million. A key parameter in this was the existence within the reinsurance contract of a 24-hour clause. This meant that the precise sequence of events, though confused, was vital to the fair and appropriate settlement of claims.

The fire plan, as drawn, showed how closely the fire followed the earthquake. The first stage was to exclude damage probably caused by the earthquake, and then damage caused by looting. Then payment was first made under policies covering earthquake damage. 'Fire only' claims were put aside until later. When the team came to deal with 'Fire only' claims, the plan worked with almost computer-like precision. A system was adopted working on the principle that the nearer in time to the earthquake the fire occurred, the more probable it was that the earthquake itself would have been the main cause. So, if the fire occurred on the day of the earthquake, 10 per cent of the fire claim would be paid; if on the second day, 20 per cent; on the third day, 30 per cent.

The population of Managua before the disaster was estimated at about 400,000. The death toll was considered to be between 10,000 and 12,000, while some 200,000 or more were rendered homeless. A major international relief effort could only mitigate the effects of the earthquake. No amount of insurance could restore the situation that existed before this disaster. Yet the system for payment of claims proved to be generally accepted as fair and reasonable.

DARWIN

Early on Christmas Day 1974 the town of Darwin in the Northern Territory of Australia was devastated by a cyclone with the inappropriately pretty name of Tracy. (Hurricanes and cyclones were in

The Darwin Cyclone, 1974.

those days given girls' names, in alphabetical order; in later years, after feminine protests, male names were added to the sequence.) Cyclones are familiar in the Pacific. Indeed, Darwin had suffered from them before, in 1889 and 1937. But not many of the inhabitants of the town, or the population of the Territory as a whole, were there forty years before, let alone in the nineteenth century. Most residents were comparative newcomers. Therefore few people ever thought of the prospect of cyclones: and the few who did no doubt viewed them with the same sense of improbability as the residents of America's west coast think of the San Andreas fault.

It was not until the last moment that it became apparent that Cyclone Tracy would hit Darwin. Cyclones are erratic and unpredictable in their movements, and it was not until shortly before midnight on Christmas Eve that it became evident that the eye of the storm would pass over the town. What happened was far worse than anyone could have predicted. Shortly before the cyclone reached the coast, the eye of the storm shrank rapidly, intensifying and increasing the already high winds in the 'maximum speed ring', a band around the eye of the cyclone. In a strange diversion, the eye of the storm did not pass over in a straight line − which would have been damaging enough − but twisted into a reverse 'S', crossing the town once, then bending back over the sea and traversing the town again. The wind speeds were estimated at over 200 mph (the anemometer at Darwin airport was demolished after recording speeds of 175 mph).

The damage was huge. It soon became clear that the insured losses in relation to domestic buildings was around Aus $100 million, and to domestic contents an additional $27.5 million. The losses of commercial buildings was smaller (since there were fewer of them, and often more strongly built), at $12.5 million, with commercial contents (including profits) at $35 million. Damage to motor vehicles was estimated at $7.5 million, and to boats and aircraft at $25 million. Other associated losses (including, for example, rent) were a further $22.5 million. The challenge facing the loss adjusters was in proportion to these immense losses.

Immediately after the cyclone, the Australian insurance market decided to act as one unified body, making special arrangements for the handling of the Darwin claims. One of the strongest arguments for this course of action was the sensitivity of the insurance business in Australia in 1974. Following the Brisbane floods, less than a year earlier, the insurers had become unpopular with both the (Labour) Government and many flood victims. This was because many policies carried an exclusion clause for flood damage, and as a result many policy-holders found too late that they were not covered against the damage to their homes. Nationalization of the insurance industry had been adopted as official Government policy.

The situation in Darwin was made doubly sensitive since many of the residents were civil servants, who had moved there at the behest of the Government to administer the expansion of the town and the Northern Territory, stimulated by the discovery of uranium ore nearby. There were also navy, army and air force defence establishments.

At first the Australian insurance market set up a bureau in Darwin, with two sections: the first would process claims, and the second would deal with surveying and adjusting. The members of these sections were drawn from personnel throughout Australia, and it was decided that each staffer would serve a ten-day stint before being replaced. This no doubt seemed reasonable in the chaotic and inhospitable conditions then prevailing in Darwin, but it soon proved inefficient. Some of the imported staff had no experience in the measurement of building or contents losses, or the management of the more severe commercial losses. They attempted to do their best in intolerable conditions, but inevitably inconsistencies were built into the system, and the ten-day handovers led to lapses in practice in dealing with the larger claims. Indeed, some of the larger claims were dealt with directly by adjusting firms outside the bureau, which was a further cause of inconsistency.

Following the cyclone a Toplis and Harding team, headed by Robert Cole, flew into Darwin to represent the British reinsurers. Already the Australian insurance market was beginning to realize that the methods of dealing with claims were not efficient. There were various reasons for this, one of them being the inexperience of some of those asked to carry out the highly technical business of loss adjusting; another was certainly that the physical devastation of Darwin, where most of the property was domestic, had obliged the surviving residents to abandon their homes and possessions and move thousands of miles to whichever of Australia's population centres would offer them shelter (the nearest State capital was Adelaide, almost two thousand miles away). Much work therefore had to be done at long distance. With the help of the President of the Australian branch of the Chartered Institute of Loss Adjusters, and following suggestions from the Toplis and Harding team, a more effective system was swiftly set up. For the following six months, forty first-class loss adjusters worked in Port Darwin for

30 days each on six and a half days a week. Each evening, the loss adjusters met to exchange experience and to discuss the schedule for the following day. On average, the adjustment of each loss took two hours, i.e. approximately 30,000 working hours. Although the personnel cost totalled US $700,000, this represented only 0.2% of the overall loss insured, a remarkably low figure. The new system enabled the adjusters to receive and handle claims, and to determine equitable settlements acceptable to those who had suffered loss, to the Australian insurance market and to the London reinsurers.

Such a stressful operation could hardly have been completed without the occasional moment of humour. Old hands in the Toplis and Harding team took a perverse pleasure in 'initiating' newcomers by practical jokes. One new arrival was met at the airport (which was fortunately still able to operate) by a car which took him to a hotel. Behind the reception desk was a caricature of an Australian, scruffy and beery. He directed the newcomer to a room on the top floor. After climbing the stairs with a heavy suitcase, after a long flight, the newcomer put the key in the door, opened it – and found himself looking into a room with no ceiling and only one wall, open to the elements. It slowly dawned on him that this was not seriously intended to be his base.

The first task was to define the damage. Most – and this was apparent from the insurance portfolios of the local companies – proved to be domestic. In the centre of the city were a few office skyscraper blocks, hotels, department stores, supermarkets, motels and restaurants, and a high proportion of government buildings. But the remainder of the city comprised suburban estates extending along the coast on both sides of the peninsula on which Darwin stands, for a distance of about 15 kilometres. These residential estates were built on flat and exposed coast; they had been built fast, and using simple light materials suitable for a warm climate in which extreme weather was unprecedented.

The greatest number of houses had been built by the Northern Territories Administration to house Commonwealth public servants. Around 6000 houses had been built, most of them single-storey, raised eight to nine feet above ground level on concrete or steel piles with timber, concrete or steel beams. The walls were asbestos fibre sheets, with timber floors and a corrugated iron roof on a timber frame. Tenants were encouraged to buy their houses, and some 4500 had done so, many of them improving the houses by enclosing the ground floor for use as storage, laundry or garaging.

The next largest section was of houses built and owned by the

Housing Commission and let to non-public servants. There were about 1300 of these houses, with 2500 flats of similar construction but in buildings of two to four storeys. Finally there were some 2000 privately built and owned houses, most of a higher structural standard, but built of a variety of materials.

Few of these houses were built to withstand cyclones. Indeed, some constructions were held together by nothing more than four-inch nails, so that a strong wind would easily take off the roof; and many walls were of such flimsy construction that flying debris punctured them and enabled the wind to sweep under the roof space.

Apart from the damage to houses, there was substantial damage to cars, to light aircraft parked at Darwin Airport, and to boats in the harbour. It was estimated that there were some 10,000 cars in the town at the time the cyclone struck, and of those, 6000 were damaged to a greater or lesser extent (many because they were parked under or beside houses demolished in the storm). Most of the aircraft at the airport were simply thrown into the air and up-ended. Some small fishing vessels put to sea at the onset of the storm in the hope of riding it out, and were never seen again.

The general conclusions of the Toplis and Harding team on this disaster highlighted the particular characteristics of the damage caused. First, Cyclone Tracy was of unusual ferocity; while gales and even cyclones are not rare on the coasts of Northern Australia, this was the first time that one had struck a populous area. Because so many residents of Darwin had moved there in comparatively recent years, few of them were aware of the perils of cyclones. As a result of this, housing construction was comparatively lightweight, as might be expected in a temperate climate. Partly as a result of this, people were careless about increasing the insured value of their homes annually, and so many properties were substantially under-insured.

This, together with the then Australian Government's active involvement in matters concerning the insurance market, added extra problems, which took many months to resolve satisfactorily. However, given the scale of the disaster, that was perhaps not surprising. The population of Darwin was about 46,000 in December 1974. The estimated insured loss estimate was Aus $230 million, giving a loss of $5000 per head of population. This was believed to be the highest per capita loss recorded in any disaster up to that time.

12. Pasta and Couscous

ANOTHER ASPECT of the valuation engineer's work is more mundane, and yet vital to the insurance market. This is the survey. Toplis and Harding have built up over the years a worldwide reputation in the technical field of survey and valuation. One such task may stand for many more. This was the survey of flour mills, pasta plants and couscous manufactories carried out in 1966 for the Algerian Government.

President de Gaulle declared Algeria independent of France on 3 July 1962. The incoming republican and revolutionary government proceeded to nationalize foreign-owned assets: all agricultural land held by foreigners had been expropriated by October 1963, and many foreign nationals left the country.

By a Decree of the Council of the Revolution dated 22 May 1964 all the flour mills, pasta plants and couscous manufactories were nationalized. Most of these had been French-owned, and there then followed the question of compensation. It was clear that this would depend upon valuation. The agents Booz Allen and Hamilton International, incorporated in London and Algiers, commissioned Toplis and Harding and Findlay (the predecessor of the modern Toplis Engineering and THESIS – Toplis and Harding Engineering Surveying and Inspection Services) to prepare a valuation on the general basis of Going Concern of the land, buildings, plant and machinery of the 66 flour mills and 20 pasta plants administered by the Société Nationale des Semouleries, Meuneries, Fabriques de Pâtes Alimentaires et Couscous (SEMPAC), the nationalized body now administering these installations.

For about six months in 1966, a Toplis and Harding and Findlay team generally of five or six people tried to come to grips with this complex and ill-documented industry. It was ill-documented because as the French managers withdrew from the country, they took with them all the drawings, inventories and schedules describing the hardware. Having identified and described the situation, the team were then asked to present a report making recommendations for compensation.

The key to this was a legal opinion obtained from Mark Littman, a leading expert on international law at the London bar. Mr Littman described the various legal precedents, and introduced the accepted formula for the expropriation of alien property: that it should be adequate, effective and prompt. In some cases it had been argued that 'adequate' compensation should mean the value of an undertaking at the moment of dispossession, plus interest to the day of judgment. In practice, however, it seemed that in many instances, 70 per cent of the value was the largest recompense achieved.

For payment to be 'effective' meant that it was in a form that could be used by the recipient. Non-transferable bonds or blocked currency would therefore not be effective in this sense. 'Promptness' was a further contentious issue. In the twenty years since the Second World War, it seemed that the shortest period in which compensation had been agreed and paid was one year and eight months from the date of a nationalization law. There seemed to be general agreement in international law that full payment could be deferred if the total amount to be paid was fixed, if interest were payable in the case of late payment, and if the guarantees for payment were strong enough for the person to be compensated to be enabled to raise funds on the security of future payment.

Following on this legal opinion, Ninian Hawken as consultant to Toplis and Harding and Findlay prepared a report defining the precise basis of valuation of the Algerian flour mills, pasta and couscous works, and making recommendations for compensation. This was done not least on the basis of British practice, because (and there is a certain irony in this during the decade of the 1980s) the British Government had in the years following the Second World War nationalized a large part of the private sector, including railways and road transport, coal mines, gas and electricity undertakings and the steel industry.

The systems of compensation had been calculated in two ways: first, in relation to companies quoted on the Stock Exchange, by reference to Stock Exchange prices (either the average of a series, or at alternative prices on specific dates). Secondly, in other cases when companies were privately owned (this was particularly the case with road transport), vehicles were valued at cost less a fixed formula laid down in an Act of Parliament for depreciation. Other assets were acquired at 'market value', defined as the price as between a 'willing buyer' and a 'willing seller'. The greater part of the compensation was in Government stock, the value of which was based on the current cost of government loan at the time of the compensation (the purpose being to restrict the inflationary effect of paying cash).

The British view of compensation payable to British nationals whose property overseas had been nationalized was that set out in the Legal Opinion – that it should be 'adequate, effective and prompt'. On 'adequacy', Hawken emphasized that compensation should be adequate as between the nationalized State and the former owners, whether the latter were comparatively poor individuals, or rich and powerful international enterprises. 'Effectiveness' meant that the compensation must be paid in a negotiable form. Finally, 'prompt' payment was probably more acceptable than just compensation, in the long run.

As to the method of payment, Hawken noted that it had been found most efficient for the nationalizing State to pay a lump sum compensation. In the Algerian case, the great majority of the former owners of flour mills and pasta and couscous works were French nationals: Hawken therefore recommended strongly that a lump sum should be paid to the French Government for them to divide up, rather than for the Algerian authorities to start complex and detailed negotiations with a number of companies and individuals. There was a double advantage in this. The paying authority would have to conduct one single transaction; and those claiming compensation would be claiming against their own government.

The report's main recommendation, then, was that a Compensation Fund should be set up, its assets to consist of five elements: the 1966 valuation of land, buildings and machinery made by the team from Toplis and Harding and Findlay, adjusted to 1964 values (the year of the expropriation decree) on the best general basis available; a small element for office furniture and household effects; vehicles, valued at cost (where known) less 20 per cent per annum depreciation; stocks in hand; and cash in hand. It was proving difficult to establish the precise amounts of stocks in hand in 1964, and the figure now proposed was 60 per cent of the value of the stocks throughout the industry at 1 May 1966.

Against these assets would be offset any local debts and obligations left behind by former owners and owed to Algerian interests, and also a global sum to cover any tax indebtedness: it was recommended that this should be dealt with globally, rather than introduce the complexities of individual tax computations.

The figure of 60 per cent of value was introduced despite the fact that in nationalizing their own electricity and gas enterprises after the war the French Government had established a figure of 70 per cent for compensation. This was to allow for the uncertainties of valuation experienced by the Toplis and Harding and Findlay team, not least the effects of the changes that had taken place between the date of the nationalization decree in 1964 and the valuation on the ground two years later. There had been some transfers of equipment, and some additions and removals of equipment, but these were considered insignificant. Local statistics were unobtainable, but it was certain that since nationalization there was no longer any market for land, and labour costs and material costs, and customs, freightage and other charges, had all risen.

It had been suggested that some mills were not capable of maintaining a normal level of profit at the time of nationalization, and that the owners were only maintaining profits by not carrying out repairs and renewals, and by illicit marketing above controlled prices. Perhaps it is not surprising that, in the circumstances, full accounts and records for the period up to 1964 were 'not available'.

With the assistance of two young engineers from Henry Simons in Stockport, the Toplis and Harding and Findlay team set out to find and itemize the various pieces of machinery. There were generally two bases for valuation: first, the fiscal cost for insurance, based on purchase price less depreciation; and secondly, the going concern value. This could pose problems.

Many picturesque mills were found of such antiquity, and of such massive and out-dated construction and equipment, as to demand employment of large numbers of the local population. Each of these old mills could only achieve at high cost a production that could have been equalled or exceeded by, say, modern four-roller milling machines tended by half-a-dozen hands, housed in light buildings. In another situation, costly water-turbines driven by river-flow, and the necessary maintenance staff, could be replaced by motors connected to an electricity power-line recently extended to the area. The difference in such cases between 'current reinstatement cost' of the existing assets, and 'cost of equivalent-performance replacement', would therefore be vast; and the economic implications could have been repugnant, no doubt (or at least bewildering), to clients committed by inflexible ideology to the principles of full employment and maximum economic performance.

The report was presented in September 1966, complete with detailed valuations of the flour mills, pasta and couscous plants. Together with its main recommendation that the compensation should be paid as a lump sum, it was accepted and implemented by the Algerian Government.

Other challenges facing the loss adjuster cannot be resolved by taking legal advice. There are two stories told by members of the Toplis and Harding staff that illustrate the sharpness of mind and eye that must be maintained in widely differing circumstances.

Towards the close of the Biafran War in West Africa, a London insurance company received a claim on a life policy taken out earlier in the same year by a businessman working in Biafra, for the sum of £50,000. His executors put forward a claim for this sum, since it was understood that the businessman had been killed in an air crash while attempting to leave the country. The insurer was not wholly convinced by the evidence adduced by the executors for the man's death, since the precise circumstances were unclear, as was the type of aircraft. The policy excluded death or disablement consequent upon the insured engaging in or taking part in naval, military or air force service or operations.

In due course, and some considerable time after the event, a member of staff of Toplis and Harding was commissioned to investigate the circumstances and report back. By this time the war was over, and it was possible to obtain some information from the files of the Nigerian Government. It was discovered that on a night in October 1967 an aircraft hi-jacked from Nigerian Airways by Biafrans had crashed while attempting to bomb Lagos. There was some uncertainty as to whether it was shot down, or whether one or more of the primitive bombs on board had exploded prematurely. Whatever the cause, all those on board the aircraft were killed. There was evidence of enquiries being made by very distinguished relatives of the businessman living in Europe, who obviously were aware that he had been on that aircraft.

So much was certain. It was established that he had been working as an agent of the Biafran Government, concerned with the disposition of large sums of cash in Switzerland, probably for the purchase of arms. However, the absence of an identifiable body, and of sworn confirmation of witnesses that the businessman had been on the aircraft, made it impossible to reach a legally watertight conclusion. By the time the enquiries were being made, potential witnesses had (in the aftermath of the war) found employment in the four corners of the earth – where they were tracked down and interviewed.

Eventually, the surviving parties reached a settlement satisfactory to them, on a basis of negotiation conducted through legal representatives.

A further case has been called 'the case of the disappearing picture'. Toplis and Harding has for many years had a concern for, and interest in, fine art. But sometimes works of art, and their owners, act in unpredictable ways.

A Lloyd's underwriter received an invitation to provide insurance cover for a painting by a great classical painter, whose work was of rapidly increasing value on the international markets. The picture was in Rome, and privately owned. The sum requested was high by any standards. The underwriter therefore asked Toplis and Harding to look into the circumstances. A senior member of the staff decided that this was a case where personal enquiries were desirable, and later the same day he was landing at Rome Airport. There he was met by the firm's local agent, who was not best pleased at the suggestion that they should forthwith drive to the suburb where the picture's owner lived.

This turned out to be a wealthy suburb with large houses in their own grounds. There seemed to be nothing odd or unusual about the house in which the picture was stored. They approached the house, and the door was opened by an elegant woman. Yes, indeed she had the picture. Just at present she was entertaining, but perhaps the next morning she would produce it for them. . . . The man from Toplis and Harding decided that he would return the following morning. He noticed that a few yards down the road were two policemen. It turned out that they were guarding the house of the city Chief of Police, and that there would be guards on duty throughout the night. The situation was explained to them, and for a consideration they agreed to keep an eye on the neighbouring house.

The next morning the man from Toplis and Harding arrived in the street, to learn from the policemen that a woman had left the house in a hurry shortly before, carrying under her arm a large rectangular parcel wrapped in brown paper. A swift telephone call to London suspended the insurance policy. Enquiries at the airport established that the woman with the painting had flown to Milan.

No more was heard of, or from her. No premium was paid on the insurance policy. The man from Toplis and Harding was left wondering how, where and when she was going to arrange for the picture to be stolen. . . .

For the teams from Toplis and Harding, the seventies were a period of considerable overseas travelling. In 1976 Wyndham Harding did a world trip that started with a board meeting in Chicago, then west to San Francisco, Honolulu, Tokyo, Manila, Taiwan, Sydney, Melbourne, Canberra and Perth, Hong Kong, Singapore and Tokyo.

For personal reasons he had to return directly to London, which was a disappointment as he had hoped to fly back through India, and see the Himalayas from the air.

Wyndham Harding.

Those flights were rather more comfortable than one endured by Robert Cole, Tom Hudson and Huw Rodge a year or two later during a visit to Venezuela to inspect an oil refinery. They chartered a light aircraft to fly them over the mountains; their pilot was a German who, they were interested to discover, had been in the Luftwaffe. The flight out was competent, despite threatening weather. It had

116

been explained that they must leave in good time to get back to Caracas, because the small local airport closed at 5.30.

As they began to climb to clear the mountains, there was extreme turbulence, thunder and lightning. It became obvious that they would not reach Caracas before 5.30, and so the pilot said that he would have to go to the international airport – which was on the other side of the mountains. At this stage he admitted that the only map he had was a local road map, and that he could not read the instruments because he had forgotten to bring his glasses. The aircraft began to climb, bucketing about the thunderous sky, and one of his passengers lay full length on the cabin floor, peering up at the instruments and reading them aloud. They tried to raise the international airport by radio, but without success. At this point the pilot admitted that he had no permission to attempt a landing there – and indeed had no licence for night flying. As it was now pitch dark, the only illumination coming from flashes of lightning, this was not encouraging.

Eventually the pilot decided that they must have crossed over the mountains, without hitting them, and so he would descend. This he did, and mercifully identified the lights of the international airport. Equally mercifully, no planes appeared to be about to land. He put down on the fringe of the airport and begged them to move out fast. He seemed to have one worry.

'You weren't frightened, were you?' he asked insistently. 'I do not like my passengers to be frightened.'

13. Rapid Transport

MANY OF the world's great engineering projects have been at the forefront of new technologies. It is almost inevitable, therefore, that there will be problems when innovation fails to deliver on time. As most of those who have worked through the 'computer revolution' are well aware, failure may be due to physical faults in materials or structure, or human misjudgment in design or execution. With the introduction of innovative technologies there are often consequential losses; and it is the function of the loss adjuster to advise the insurers on the validity of claims within the terms of policies as drawn.

The following cases in the late 1970s may represent a number with which Toplis and Harding have been concerned.

Bay Area Rapid Transit (San Francisco).

The motor car has turned into both a blessing and a curse to city dwellers of the twentieth century. The city of San Francisco is among the first to discover the problems caused by the car in modern urban planning. The business centre of San Francisco is built on a peninsula curving round the western side of San Francisco Bay. There is therefore no scope for building development other than upwards. The centre of the city is linked to its eastern and northern suburbs by two great bridges, Oakland Bay (built in 1936) and the more famous Golden Gate bridge (completed in 1937). The first gives access to the city from Oakland (and the University of California at Berkeley); the second links it to Marin County to the north.

Before the bridges were built, ferries brought 50 million passengers a year to the foot of Market Street. By 1970, a quarter of a million cars per day were coming into the city over the bridges (to which were added the cars driving up the peninsula from the bedroom suburbs of San Mateo to the south). The traffic congestion was horrendous, and so was the damage these exhaust fumes were doing to the atmosphere, and to the lungs of citizens. San Francisco was the centre of a metropolitan area of nine counties, home to more than 4 million people. It had suffered natural disasters, such as the great earthquake and fire of 1906 (which was to be repeated, though on a mercifully smaller scale, in 1989). But the main problems of modern San Francisco were man-made; and so would be the solution.

San Francisco had been the main springboard for the departure of American troops during the war in the Pacific in the 1940s. The problems caused in dealing with these great numbers of men and machines emphasized the need to provide better transport across the Bay. By the 1970s there were half a million commuters travelling in and out of San Francisco each day. The remit was to carry large numbers of people from the suburbs, many across the Bay, fast and safely into central San Francisco, and to return them home in the evening. So the concept of the Bay Area Rapid Transit (BART) System was created, by the San Franciso Bay Area Rapid Transit District Act of 1957. It was to be almost 20 years before the system came into operation.

The delays were caused by all the complications of planning within a highly congested urban area, the conflicts of interest adding to the huge structural problems. Initially it had been intended that five local counties would participate; by the mid-sixties, the number had reduced to three – San Francisco, Alameda and Contra Costa. The constructors examined as many modern forms of mass transit as they could discover – buses, ferries, hydrofoils, railways – and chose a light railway. In the early stages it was thought possible that the railway might run over the Golden Gate Bridge, but the managers refused to entertain that proposal. Instead, it was agreed that BART would cross the bay in a submarine tube of steel, four miles long.

There were to be 34 stations, some elevated, some at ground level, some in subways. The aim was to transport 200,000 passengers per day, or 30,000 per hour, on modern 'subway' cars travelling at up to 80 mph. They would travel 90 seconds apart at peak hours in trains of two to ten cars. It was subsequently decided that the system would be wholly computer-controlled, at a cost of $26 million for the Automatic Train Control (ATC) developed by the leading electronics manufacturer, Westinghouse. In November 1962 the voters of the three counties concerned authorized – by narrow majorities – the issue by the District of $792 million in bonds for the construction of the BART system.

The complexities of the construction contracts were naturally considerable. They went to a consortium of three major companies, Parsons Brinckerhoff-Tudor-Bechtel, together with Rohr Industries for the supply of transit vehicles and Westinghouse for the control system. Building began, and the first section of track opened for public use on 11 September 1972 in southern Alameda, a country line from Fremont to MacArthur Station in Oakland. Two years later, on 16 September 1974, the first trains began to run under the Bay.

It seems strange, looking back over the mere 15 years in which BART has become an essential part of the travel scene in San Francisco, to comprehend the problems that attended the first few years, and led to substantial litigation (the most famous case of which was a Class Action brought by Milton Stern jun. for $100 million in the San Francisco Supreme Court).

That there were teething troubles is beyond doubt. Within a month of the public opening of the first stretch of track, a two-car train 'suddenly and without warning accelerated to a speed of approximately 66 mph in an area of track where the maximum designed speed limit was 27 mph'. This caused the train to go out of control; it went off the end of the track and through a sandpile and fence, severely damaging the undercar equipment and the car frame. The fault was alleged to be due to a component failure. Passengers in the cars suffered injuries. A writ issued at the time assesssed damage to the cars and track at $412,075.50, and assessed the cost of personal injury actions and expenses at $1.5 million, a total of just under $2 million.

In November 1974 a faulty electrical connection caused the friction brakes on one car to operate intermittently, building up heat that eventually caused a fire that destroyed the car. A still more serious accident occurred in January 1975, when the train detection equipment, a key element in the automatic train control, apparently failed to detect a maintenance truck on the line, with the result that it was struck by a train. One BART employee was killed, two others were injured, the train, track and wayside equipment were severely damaged and the maintenance vehicle was destroyed. Trains were given information by trackside control equipment. In February 1976 there was a defect in one of these trackside control boards that caused a car to be given the wrong speed information: this caused it to enter the Fremont Station too fast, and the train attendant had to apply the override and stop it.

There were problems with the doors of some of the cars. There were reports of doors opening when the cars were moving, doors opening on the wrong side when the train came into a station, and even of doors opening when trains were still entering a station. It was further claimed that the doors of the 450 cars were not interchangeable, which suggested additional costs in maintenance.

These matters all went before the courts. The various parties made claims, largely with Lloyd's of London. The satisfactory resolution of the insurance problems kept Toplis and Harding Inc. in San Francisco extremely busy. Their Vice-President, Jim Young, led the team assessing this very large and complex operation.

Many other challenging assignments were dealt with by the American company in those years. Chris Stafford recalls three in particular. One concerned riots that broke out in several federal and state penitentiaries, leading to huge property damage and loss of lives. One, in a maximum security jail at Santa Fe, New Mexico, was particularly brutal. Evidently due to overcrowding, the prisoners rioted without any previous indication that trouble was imminent. The State of New Mexico held replacement cost cover for damage to buildings resulting from riot, and actual cash value coverage on equipment. There was also a form of extra expense cover providing time element coverage. The determination of the property loss was predicated upon estimated costs of repair or replacement. There was an additional and unusual element of claim, which was the State's argument of a 'Sue and Labor' expense for calling out the National Guard to quell the riot. The State contended that the cost of the National Guard was incurred to prevent further physical damage. Underwriters at Lloyd's were involved, as well as American domestic insurers.

The second case was that of a floating bridge owned by the State of Washington, in the Pacific North-west of the United States. There are in fact four large concrete bridges constructed with a unique floating structure design. The base of the roadways is carried on huge pontoons which float on the water. The pontoons, resembling large barges, have hatch openings so that the interiors can be inspected periodically. Each opening has a metal hatch cover which when closed is held in place by a latch device. By an unfortunate coincidence, all the hatch covers had been removed for maintenance shortly before a severe winter storm. Though they had been returned before the storm, more maintenance was required on the latches, and so the covers were not properly secured. During the storm, the pontoons were buffeted by waves, and water swept over them, lifting the hatch covers and flooding the pontoons so that the roadway and superstructure sank. The bridge was partly insured on an all-risk physical loss basis; and although the insurers questioned the fortuity of the loss, the State of Washington was partially indemnified for the resulting loss.

The third case concerned a dam on the Guri River in Venezuela. Within the main section of the dam, there were sluiceways or portals that were equipped with massive steel inserts. The construction design called for the sluiceways to be closed at the same time as the reservoir was being filled. However, when the steel inserts were being lowered into position to close the portals, several of the steel gates jammed and could not be lowered or raised. The reservoir filled to such a height that the water poured through the openings, and there was a threat that the force of the water might endanger the whole structure. A 'Sue and Labor' claim was instigated while the builders tried vainly to plug the openings by lowering huge boulders cabled together, and other materials, from the top of the dam. This failed to work and eventually it was necessary to build an earth coffer dam in front of the open portals. This enabled workers to descend into the sluiceways and free the jammed metal gates. In time, the portals were secured and the insurers, Lloyd's underwriters, made a contribution to the 'Sue and Labor' protection expense.

Sometimes the 'knock-on' effect of a disaster leads to claims that could hardly have been predicted at the outset. Drake Ratcliffe of Toplis and Harding Inc. recalls one extraordinary series of consequences in a disaster off the coast of Spain.

A vessel bound from Amsterdam to the East carrying a cargo of chemicals had a major explosion in the boiler room. Many crew were killed. The vessel washed onto rocks off the Spanish coast. Some of the chemicals fell into the sea and reacted with sea water to form a gas cloud, causing residents on the nearby shoreline to be evacuated. Some chemicals, intact in their containers, were washed ashore. The Government sent lorries, manned by police, to pick up the chemicals from the beach. This was done, and then the Government had to find

The Guri River Dam, Venezuela.

123

somewhere to dispose of them. The convoy of three lorries wound its way through the local province for five days, and meanwhile the popular clamour from the media described the cargo as injurious to health, and even as being of nuclear waste. Everywhere the trucks arrived they were met by local people determined to turn them away.

Finally the Government decided to off-load the chemicals on to ships, using the deep water harbour of the local aluminium plant. When the trucks arrived at the plant gates, the workers advised the management that if the trucks were permitted to enter, the workers would immediately strike. Negotiations began, and eventually it seemed that the workers might be persuaded to allow the loading to take place. But then, for no obvious reason, the lorries, which had been parked a mile away, started up and began to move towards the plant gates. Seeing the lorries approaching, the workers downed tools and left.

The management was unable to maintain operations, and the aluminium pot lines went cold, causing huge damage. The damage to the aluminium pot lines was the subject of the insurance claim.

Many other American cases involved natural disasters. Two memorable cases followed from floods. One concerned the breaching of a dyke at the Great Salt Lake, and as a result the flooding of 19,000 acres of solar evaporation ponds, causing a major physical loss and a business interruption claim that continued for almost seven years.

Another flood damaged a trout farm. The trout were being raised for commercial purposes in a man-made pond or lake through which naturally flowing river water was diverted. When the river flooded beyond all previous experience, it wiped out the trout-raising facility and the fish were either destroyed or swam away.

Finally there was the case that followed the destruction of a chicken farm in the path of a tornado. High winds destroyed several barns, each housing 25,000 birds who were there for egg production. Most of the birds survived, and many were later captured, but were lost as egg producers because the traumatic experience of the tornado caused them to moult and to stop laying for 30 days. It was uneconomical to feed such a large number of unproductive birds for such a long period, and they were killed. The farmer claimed a business interruption loss, arguing that the chickens were production equipment.

14. Years of Expansion

THE EARLY 1980s were a challenging time for the Toplis and Harding partnership, as for many other similar firms in the service industries. The difficulties were partly caused by the problems of success and expansion. The introduction of new technology (as so often) proved to cost more than had been estimated. Computers and word-processors took longer to demonstrate their positive economies than had been planned. The purchase of a company in Papua New Guinea, aimed at strengthening Toplis and Harding representation in the Far East, required a rapid injection of funds. More money was needed to buy out the minority shareholders in the Toplis and Harding company in Switzerland.

There was expansion at home. Toplis and Harding Marine moved into larger offices at Barking, Essex, and marine arms were added to the Dublin and Manchester offices, and subsequently to Belfast. The move out of central London was continued when Toplis and Harding and Partners moved to Enfield. In 1980 new offices were opened in Aberdeen, Brighton, Haverfordwest and Gravesend. In 1981, an office was opened in Scunthorpe. In Ireland, Walter Hume became a limited liability company and opened new branches in County Tipperary and Sligo.

Abroad, Toplis and Harding International was obliged to close its Iran office (following the revolution) and also that in Beirut (in the early days of the internal wars). But new offices were opened in Panama, Bridgetown, Nicosia, Nairobi and Mombasa. In 1981 Toplis and Harding and Partners changed its name once more to Toplis and Harding Technical and formed its own international company.

The reputation of Toplis and Harding was high, and nowhere more so than in the Middle East, increasingly prosperous through oil revenues (an office was opened in Dubai, following the success of the Kuwait office). It was therefore no surprise, and in the challenging financial circumstances not unwelcome, when overtures were made by Middle East financial sources to take an interest in the partnership.

As a result of many months of discussion and negotiation, on 26 May 1982 all the partnerships within the Toplis and Harding Group disposed of 80 per cent of their interest to Resources Management Corporation (RMC) and the Sharjah Investment Corporation. The latter organization was represented by the Sharjah Investment Co. (UK) Ltd, which had been formed in 1976 and incorporated as a public company with offices in the Gulf, Kuwait and London. It was the first company of its kind, and included amongst its founding shareholders some of the most important high net-worth individuals in the Gulf, including some members of the Kuwait ruling family. While the Kuwait and Gulf offices were primarily concerned with the infrastructure of that area, the London office acted as a conduit for the group in the international markets.

For the purpose of this sale, the original Toplis and Harding partnerships were wound up and changed to limited liability companies. The group parent company was Toplis and Harding (International) Holdings Ltd, of which RMC held 56 per cent of the shares, Sharjah 24 per cent and the former partners 20 per cent. The overseas wing consisted of Toplis and Harding (International) Ltd and Toplis and Harding Technical (International) Ltd. The home side operated under a subordinate holding company, Toplis and Harding Holdings (UK) Ltd with sister operating companies, Toplis and Harding UK Ltd, Toplis and Harding Marine Ltd, and Toplis and Harding Technical Ltd. The last, which was principally concerned with valuation work, changed its name to Appraisal and Valuation Consultants (AVC). Toplis and Harding (Arabia) Ltd was formed, 90 per cent owned by RMC/Sharjah and 10 per cent by Toplis and Harding (International) Holdings Ltd, adding to the old offices in Dubai and Kuwait new offices in Saudi Arabia at Jeddah, Riyadh and Al Khobar, and another at Muscat, Oman. The Toplis and Harding office in Nicosia, Cyprus, also became part of this company. Toplis and Harding Marine also began to expand abroad, with marine surveyor attachments to the Toplis and Harding offices in Hong Kong and Jeddah. As part of the general business pattern of moving offices out of the increasingly expensive City, the engineering division was relocated at Rickmansworth.

Two new companies were formed in this period: Technical Audit, a consultancy company specializing in providing services to the process plant and manufacturing industries to ensure that their plant and equipment operate reliably, efficiently and safely; and Quaestor Services.

In the 1980s there were considerable changes in the representation

126

of Toplis and Harding in the United States. In 1980 Ted Persson, President (chief executive) of Toplis and Harding Inc., decided to retire; the consequent withdrawal of the considerable Persson family holdings presented some difficulties to the remaining partners. It was the company secretary, Walter B. Remdt, who found a financial 'godfather' in the shape of the Employers' Reinsurance Corporation of Kansas City which, after prolonged negotiations, purchased Toplis and Harding Inc. and appointed Wally Remdt as President. There were then 13 Toplis and Harding offices across the States, and in addition the Canadian offices. As not infrequently happens after such events, there followed a series of departures in unhappy circumstances.

Donald Maxson, head of the Los Angeles office, received an offer to join the rival company Graham Miller, which he accepted, as did his colleague Jim Young: from 1981 they began an American operation in the name of Graham Miller.

In 1983 Lloyd's of London were facing problems concerning the slow settlement of claims, particularly in the United States. The reputation of Lloyd's in the insurance market was unrivalled in the States, as elsewhere; but repeated failures to settle claims speedily was losing business. The Chairman of Lloyd's initiated a campaign to get claims settled faster. Thereafter, the Non-Marine Association at Lloyd's expressed an interest in bidding for Toplis and Harding Inc., because it seemed possible that such a corporation, well known to their market for many years, might form the basis of a Lloyd's settlement office in the USA.

With the permission of the Committee and Council of Lloyd's, the deal was concluded and a management committee was formed at Lloyd's, headed by the Chairman of Toplis and Harding Inc. (THI), Michael H. Cockell, who was chairman of the Non-Marine Association at the time (and who fittingly had a still older connection with Toplis and Harding in the States, since his father had been one of the earliest contacts of Graham Harding, who had been Michael Cockell's godfather, together with Henry Glidden).

Unfortunately the Lloyd's direct involvement in the company did not prove successful, and in 1988 Lloyd's divested itself of the company through a management buy-out. It did not prove possible for the parent company of Toplis and Harding in London to reacquire their former American branch, and therefore the somewhat invidious situation arose that Toplis and Harding Inc. in the United States trades independently of, and dissociated from, the Toplis and Harding Group in the United Kingdom.

127

However, Toplis and Harding (UK) were able to buy from Inchcape, its then owner, the Graham Miller Company in the United States, which was being run by the former Toplis and Harding men, Donald Maxson and Jim Young. Under the name of Maxson Young Associates they thus rejoined their former colleagues to become the North American Division of the Toplis and Harding Group, with special responsibility for operations in the United States, Canada and Mexico. The head office is in San Francisco, with other offices throughout the USA.

Following the tragic death of Donald Maxson in 1988 while working on the aftermath of Hurricane Gilbert in Jamaica, Jim Young took over as Chairman of Maxson Young Associates, with Chris Stafford as President. Others from Toplis and Harding Inc. to join Maxson Young were Ray DePole, Jim Reed, Jim Donovan and Russ York. The Hurricane Gilbert operation, in fact, brought Maxson Young Associates back into a working team with colleagues from Toplis UK and Toplis International.

The early 1980s had been relatively free from major disasters, with the notable exceptions of Hurricane Allen which struck the East Caribbean in 1980, the flooding in Spain that caused $60,000,000 of damage at the Alcan plant in Alicante, and Cyclone Oscar which caused major destruction in Fiji, both in 1983. In the work following the cyclone, teams from the London and Australian offices assisted the local and reinsurance market. Another natural disaster was to provide Toplis and Harding with another 'first' in 1986, when Typhoon Vera (known locally as Typhoon 13) devastated the Democratic People's Republic of North Korea. A team from Toplis and Harding, Roger Schwab and Tom Hudson, visited North Korea in the following December to examine claims on behalf of the re-insurers. This was the first job done by Toplis and Harding in a Communist country. Another Toplis and Harding team was working in South Korea at the time.

Two provinces took the worst of the effects of the typhoon, Kangwon and North Hangyong. Some evidence of the scale of the damage may be gauged from the fact that several areas received a third of their usual annual rainfall in three days; and as the storm passed along the coast, there was associated damage from high tides and flooding. The Toplis and Harding team were able to see for themselves the damage done to the main four-lane highway from Pyongyang, the capital, to Wonsan, which had suffered from severe landslips in many places, and a number of bridges had been washed away. Another severely devastated area was around the Ryongda dam, which burst, washing away two entire neighbouring villages.

The road was not insured. Most of the insured premises were factories, schools, sanatoriums, principal stores and some dwellings. The total insured losses were valued at something over £27 million, of which 455 represented total losses, and 527 partial losses. The Toplis and Harding team were given open access to a number of damaged areas, and to the manually-kept records of the local insurance officials. They were able to report on the high standard achieved by all personnel in coping with this national disaster.

In 1984 a major disaster that brought international publicity was caused by the bomb planted by the IRA in the Grand Hotel at Brighton during the Conservative Party Conference in October, causing loss of life and considerable damage. That year there was also a major fire at Cricklewood. Toplis and Harding dealt with the aftermath of both events.

The winter of 1984/85 was particularly severe in Britain, bringing many insurance claims for damage caused by burst pipes. Abroad, Fiji was again struck by cyclones – a total of four: Eric in January, Nigel later that month, Gavin in March, followed by Hina. These led to some 2000 claims, and losses in the order of $100,000,000. The Australian offices were kept busy with flooding in Sydney, a hailstorm in Brisbane, and bush fires in Perth. A new office was opened by Toplis and Harding in Chile on 3 March 1985, to be plunged almost immediately into the consequences of a major earthquake. Apart from handling losses locally, in London Toplis and Harding represented the reinsurance market and assisted with funding operations, as was also done for the Fiji disaster.

In 1984 the turnover of the UK adjusting arm of the Toplis and Harding group topped £4,000,000. In 1950 the number of professional staff employed was 25: in 1985 they numbered 484.

But this was only the beginning of a period of substantial growth and change. In 1986 the Toplis and Harding Group was sold by RMC to Abaco Investment plc, a company listed on the London Stock Exchange that was making a name for itself by investing in companies providing professional services, including estate agents and insurance brokers. Two years later Abaco Investment became a wholly-owned subsidiary of British & Commonwealth Holdings plc.

On 1 July 1987 the Toplis and Harding Group merged with another large British loss adjusting firm – Trundle, Heap and Baker, transforming the company into one of the largest loss adjusting groups in the world (a brief history of Trundle, Heap and Baker is given in Appendix II). Naturally it took some time and determination to merge the various offices 'on the ground', but unity was tested early, and largely achieved, under the particular stresses and challenges of the flood of claims following the 'Great Storm' that devastated the south of England in October 1987. Toplis UK – as the home business is now called, as a division of the Toplis and Harding Group – acts for Lloyd's, the composite and specialist insurance companies, and captive and self-insuring bodies such as British Gas, the Electricity Generating Boards and the Water Authorities.

Yet another large step was taken in January 1988 when Wm. Elmslie & Son was acquired, and combined within the other marine activities within the Toplis and Harding Group, under the name of Toplis Elmslie Marine (a brief history of Wm. Elmslie & Son and its associated companies is given in Appendix III).

A major restructuring of the Toplis and Harding Group followed as a result of these acquisitions. A new senior management team was put in place in late 1988. New managing-directors were appointed to head the newly constituted divisions within the modernized structure, and a Group Chief Executive, M. J. Millor, was brought in from the insurance market.

The year was also one of considerable change on the international scene. New offices were opened in Athens and Thessalonika, Greece, and in Dar es Salaam, Tanzania and Kingston, Jamaica. The number of staff overseas now exceeded 400, more than half of them being professional adjusters or surveyors. During the year Toplis International were appointed Lloyd's and ILU Agents in Tanzania, and as a result held all such agencies throughout East Africa.

Business expanded beyond loss adjusting, in answer to the demands of the insurance market. New ventures included pre-risk surveys and loss prevention programmes. In East Africa the firm was appointed on two cargo loss prevention programmes, the first for Zambia State Insurance, relating to all imports to Zambia passing through the port at Dar es Salaam in Tanzania. The second was for the Association of Kenya Insurers and involved all imports of goods to Kenya through the port at Mombasa and the inland container port at Embakasi. The Singapore office continued to remain involved in claims arising under the Project Insurance Policy for the construction of the Singapore Mass Rapid Transit system. Project appointments were secured on new contracts in Sri Lanka, Hong Kong and the Netherlands.

The most significant event of 1988 was the devastation wreaked by Hurricane Gilbert in September 1988, particularly to the island of Jamaica. Toplis and Harding eventually dealt with some 3000 claims arising out of this hurricane, such instructions coming from a broad cross-section of both the local and international markets. To a lesser extent, Toplis and Harding were actively involved in adjusting losses in the Cayman Islands arising from the same catastrophe, with claims up to $15,000,000. Toplis and Harding personnel spent some 221 man days in Jamaica, and at the busiest period there were 35 adjusters operating on the island.

In September 1990, a management buy-out of the company was successfully completed, once again making The Toplis and Harding Group the world's largest, and oldest, independent loss adjusting firm.

Soho Square after the 'Great Storm', October 1987.

131

15. The Group in 1990

SINCE THE beginning, 200 years ago, The Toplis and Harding Group has grown to be amongst the world's largest claims handling organizations. During the latter part of this century, there has been rapid growth and some diversification into professional claims services. However, the central and most important of the Group's activities remains the adjustment of claims on behalf of the world insurance markets. Today The Toplis and Harding Group employs approximately 1000 people in 143 offices spread throughout the world. The World Headquarters is in London, within a few minutes' walk of Lloyd's.

In 1989, in order to fulfil the corporate aim of providing quality claims services that will satisfy the wants and needs of clients and their customers, the Group was restructured into various Divisions. At the same time a new 'corporate identity' was introduced to create a consistent image for all aspects of the Group and its activities. Designed by the Jenkins Group, the house style incorporates a mark or logo, a seal device showing a seated figure signifying authority and judgement reinforced by the surrounding motto, 'Integrity & Equity'.

Of the Divisions of The Toplis and Harding Group, Toplis International provide professional services to both local and international insurance markets in all aspects of claims handling arising from fire, accident, contractors all risks, liability and special risks and marine policies outside the United Kingdom and North America.

Apart from a traditional role as loss adjusters, many of the offices have expanded their activities to encompass other services required in world insurance markets. These include pre-risk surveys and loss prevention programmes. This Division now operates out of 54 offices staffed by more than 400 of its own personnel, with over half of them being professional adjusters, surveyors and engineers.

Toplis Elmslie Marine is the marine division of The Toplis and Harding Group. Toplis Elmslie Marine trades as four Divisions, each with its own speciality:

Wm Elmslie & Son, incorporating Danson Finlason Loftus and May: average adjusting (see Appendix III for the history of these companies)

Elmslie Toplis Energy: offshore and energy claims, adjusting losses involving oil and gas installations, platforms, rigs and pipelines

Elmslie Services: legal and agency services, marine liability, products liability, and contractual liability

Toplis Marine: cargo surveys and loss investigations with a specialist sub-division (Pulp and Paper) concentrating on surveying for the paper making and printing industries.

To support these activities, Toplis Elmslie Marine has a staff of diverse and highly professional personnel which includes qualified member of the Association of Average Adjusters, Barristers, Associates of the Chartered Insurance Institute, Master Mariners and Naval Architects.

The international network of The Toplis and Harding Group of companies further enables Toplis Elmslie Marine to provide a world-wide prompt and efficient service to its clients.

Toplis Insurance Services was established as a specialist Division for all non-adjusting units of the Group. One of the units, T.I.S., provides claims management and handling expertise to clients in the UK and throughout the world. The Unit is designed to provide a full claims service and is staffed and controlled by personnel trained in both insurance and legal disciplines.

The expertise of the Unit extends to the provision of all supervisory functions including policy and reinsurance contract interpretation, investigation of cases in dispute up to settlement and the need to comply with regulatory or statutory requirements. These services are offered worldwide through the Group's offices.

Another of the specialist units of the Division provides engineering consultancy in all fields of industry and commerce. All personnel are qualified in engineering generally and many have their own areas of expertise. All are available to work in any part of the world, not only with The Toplis and Harding Group but also for and on behalf of those requiring the services of engineers with the background and connections of world insurance.

The directors and staff within the Unit are generally Chartered Engineers, representing a broad and balanced spectrum of engineering disciplines and sectors including mechanical, marine, petroleum, chemical, electrical, instrument, aeronautical, process and production. Toplis Engineering personnel are widely experienced in the design, operation, maintenance, repair and reinstatement of oil and gas installations both on-shore and off-shore, petrochemical and process plant, nuclear, iron and steel, mechanical handling, power generation, paper, sugar and food processing, computer and electronic installations etc. They are able to apply non-destructive testing techniques as necessary and are familiar with the statutory requirements of cranes, lifting gear, boilers and pressure vessels.

Claims Investigation –

A consultancy service is provided to assist with the technical aspects of insurance claims investigation. The work is carried out by the Division's staff of engineers and, when necessary, in conjunction with specialist independent consultants and laboratories.

Risk Surveys –

Risk and loss prevention surveys are carried out by THESIS, another Unit of the Division, for British, European, American and other insurers, insureds and brokers of industrial or commercial subjects. The assessment of Estimated Maximum Loss, hazard analysis, provision of recommendations for risk improvement, safety audits etc. all form part of this aspect of the Division's activities. From time to time staff act as insurance consultants to government bodies, for whom surveys and reports are provided on the fixed assets of major industrial risks, the adequacy of safety arrangements and insurance cover.

Construction, Inspection and Condition Surveys –

Construction projects of all kinds are monitored with regard to quality, compliance with specifications, progress etc. This service can be of value to insurers, to purchasers or prospective purchasers of equipment. Staff are familiar with the various design and construction codes, for example BS, ASME, DIN, JIS.

The engineers forming the Divison are resident within The Toplis and Harding Group offices both in the UK and overseas. There is also a nucleus of specialists based in London who travel extensively as required.

Toplis Engineering has offices in London, Bristol and Manchester. Overseas it is represented in the Middle East, the Far East, the Caribbean and South America, Australia and Africa.

Toplis UK is a broadly based organization operating out of some 50 strategically located offices, all of which are under the day-to-day control of regional directors. The offices have a wide range of expertise available to handle all forms of losses with a staff of over 400, the majority of whom are professionally qualified.

Specialist teams are available for immediate attendance at all major losses, under the control of a director, with expertise available in engineering, surveying and construction, business interruption and stock control, with a full range of local back-up staff.

The Division has five specialist claims units:

The Agricultural Unit –

The Agricultural Unit comprises specialist staff operating from ten locations in the UK, dealing with claims arising from live-stock and horses, deadstock and growing crops, poultry and fish farming. The Unit also deals with grain silos, agricultural and aquacultural machinery. Livestock can also be lost other than as a result of insurable events and the Unit can be involved in claims arising from disease and negotiations with the Ministry of Agriculture Fisheries and Food, arguments and litigation between vendor and purchaser, and accidents to horses, exotic birds, fish and livestock generally. In-house legal expertise is available for recoveries against responsible parties in co-operation with the Unit's veterinary specialists.

The Fine Art Unit –

The Fine Art Unit deals with losses involving antiques and works of art of all categories. The Unit's specialists in the field are well-known to the market and have detailed knowledge of English and Continental furniture, clocks, toys and lead soldiers, silver, pictures, antique books, guns, mechanical musical instruments, carpets and tapestries, English, European and oriental porcelain, glassware, bronzes, netsukes and ivories, cameras, scientific instruments and collections of stamps and other ephemera. Substantial losses or damage involving jewellery are also dealt with by the Unit's staff.

The Interruption Unit –

This Unit was formed to deal specifically with business interruption losses throughout the UK with the expertise being available for use overseas if required. Losses handled include all forms of stock reconciliation claims and consequential loss claims following serious damage to commercial and industrial premises. The Unit is involved in accountancy problems generally and deals with claims arising from legal liability under professional negligence against accountants and other financial advisers. The Unit also advises on cost savings associated with risk management and damage control measures in commerce and production.

The Liability Unit –

This Unit comprises 24 specialist personnel including eight directors, based throughout regions of the UK including Northern Ireland. All types of liability claims are handled including personal injury (both third party and employers liability), property damage and losses arising from the supply of defective goods or materials. Procedures are tailor-made to individual clients' requirements. Supporting the Unit are in-house legally qualified personnel providing support on claims to the adjusting and marine Divisions when required.

The Transit Unit –

The Transit Unit was formed to handle all types of losses by road, rail, air and sea. Staffed by suitably qualified personnel the Unit has branches serving all the major seaports and container terminals, both inland and on the coast. Claims are handled for both domestic and international transit under CMR/RHA and other contract forms.

Toplis Construction is a specialist Division within The Toplis and Harding Group providing claims handling services in those fields of industry and commerce that are directly or indirectly connected with construction both in the UK and abroad. A significant proportion of the staff are Chartered Surveyors or Chartered Engineers with their own areas of expertise specifically linked with the construction industry. This specialized adjusting service has been a prominent feature of the Group's activities for many years.

The skills required to investigate losses occurring under legal liability insurances are retained, including third party and products and professional indemnity. Claim negotiations and recoveries can be undertaken and in all cases steps are taken to protect the interests of insurers. The adjusters seconded to the Division operate from the Head Office base at Heron Quay and include qualified and experienced staff in Toplis UK as well as from other Divisions in the Group.

A full claims investigation and adjustment service is given, from initial instruction to final settlement. Where appropriate, specialist independent consultants and laboratories may be instructed to investigate specific aspects of individual losses. Construction pre-risk and loss prevention surveys relating to the insurance requirement of the various forms of contract in general use in the construction industry can be undertaken by qualified Surveyors within the Division, who will provide an assessment of EMI, an analysis of hazard and recommendations for risk improvement where appropriate. The staff of the Division can participate in the drawing up of claims handling procedures.

Appendix I

Fire and Other Losses Overseas

BY D. R. D. BUCKHAM, F.C.I.L.A.

W HAT I hope to do in this paper is impart some of the colour and flavour of work overseas. Most of our work is found in the British Commonwealth, the Middle East, and in Europe, and although other cases occur from time to time almost throughout the remainder of the globe it is with these three areas that we are principally concerned. But even so, one of the most dangerous pitfalls in dealing with overseas claims is to form judgments and found decisions purely on UK standards – to assume that the mind of an Iranian lawyer will operate in the same way as that of his counterpart in the Temple; that an Indian will build a block of flats in the same way as a British contractor; and that a Chinese has studied Spicer & Pegler and keeps his books accordingly. Conditions overseas are not the same as those in the UK, and the people are different in their behaviour and thinking. It follows therefore that the pattern of claims is different, and the approach to the adjustment of the claims must be different accordingly.

Let me give an illustration. I once met in the Caribbean an agent of a British insurer who was very vocal over a misunderstanding of this kind which had lost him an account. He was concerned with some minor fire damage to a printing machine. If the damage had occurred in London it could have been repaired for about £150. But there was nobody on the island, or in the whole area, who understood these machines. The agent pointed this out to London, and said that although the damage was small the machine was a total loss, as it could not be mended and it was not economic to ship

This paper was given before the Insurance Institute of London on 25 February 1963. Reprinted by permission from the Journal of the Chartered Insurance Institute, London, vol. 62 (1965), pp. 81–96.

it long distances for repairs. Unfortunately the London office could not conceive this state of affairs, and consulted a printing engineer in the UK who repeated the figure of £150. The office then wrote back to the agent insisting that there *must* be somebody who could work on the machine; that when he had done so, the cost would be £150; and that this amount should be tendered to the insured. But of course the agent was perfectly right. There was nobody within thousands of miles capable of making repairs. The London office finally accepted this, but took a very long time before it did so and agreed to a total loss. These misunderstandings of local conditions created a great deal of bad feeling, and the business was lost.

My first experience of an overseas fire was in India. I had been posted to Bombay, and when I had been there only two days my more experienced colleague had to go to Burma to investigate some riot claims. Immediately afterwards a cable arrived instructing me to go to Assam, where the manager's bungalow on a tea estate was reported to have burned down. So I sent a telegram to the manager saying that I would arrive on a certain aircraft in three days' time, and would he very kindly meet me?

The distance of this trip was about the same as between London and Warsaw, but I reached the Assam airstrip without incident apart from the usual inconveniences of having to catch aircraft at five o'clock in the morning and the uncertainties of circling jungle airfields *en route* whilst small boys drove cows from the runways. However, the tea estate manager was not there to meet me, so I obtained a lift to the nearest township to make a telephone call. But there were no telephones at all; and I also made the unhappy discovery that telegrams from Bombay took about six days to arrive. There were no taxis and no hotels, but a train was expected some time that day which would take me to within ten miles of my destination. So I went to the railway station, and having sent off another telegram sat there for ten unhappy hours amid unfamiliar smells. The train arrived at half-past ten, and I got to my destination at half-past two in the morning. There was still nobody about, so I picked up my bag and set off to walk the last ten miles. But I had been going for only five minutes when the lights of a truck approached, and it was the manager's assistant. He was horrified to find me on the road, and immediately afterwards I was horrified to have been there, for there were two man-eating tigers in the district and they had had about fifteen victims already. Anyhow, I had arrived; and I believe that meeting the insured at 2.30 a.m. still constitutes a record.

Whilst I was learning about Eastern travel and communications by hard experience my colleague was having a more adventurous time in Burma. He was trying to reach a tin mine of which the buildings had been raided and burned by dacoits, and he too reached the nearest airstrip, but without knowing how he was going to travel the next forty miles, as the whole area was in a state of complete lawlessness and overrun with dacoits who had cut all the telegraph lines. However, the mine manager happened to be at the airstrip, and my colleague drove with him to his bungalow. No sooner had they arrived than there was another raid, with a great deal of shooting and shouting. When matters got a little quieter my colleague felt it would only be right for him to meet the people who were responsible for the damage he had gone to see, to enable him to give proper consideration to the conditions and exclusions of the policy. So eight tough-looking Burmese were invited into the bungalow and a most friendly session ensued, in which a varied selection of old rifles and shot-guns were passed over for inspection. Everybody had a drink, and the dacoits announced that they knew very well who my colleague was, even though he had arrived unheralded in the territory only two hours before: he was the insurance man. Finally the leader presented to my colleague a very handsome hand-made sheath knife which he was wearing and which had been admired. That night there was another raid on the mine, and it was necessary to evacuate into the jungle. On his return to the bungalow my colleague found that much of his baggage had been stolen; and also his new sheath knife.

Some days later, in another part of Burma, this same colleague and his interpreter were captured by about fifty angry-looking men who were carrying almost every conceivable type of firearm, including a Boys anti-tank rifle. They were marched through the jungle and taken to headquarters, though whose headquarters it was nobody knew. In those days there were 'rebels', 'Communists', and 'dacoits', but the dividing line was never very clear. Anyhow, they were brought before the head man, where they explained that they were trying to assess the damage in a nearby rubber factory which had been burned out and abandoned. This time the bush telegraph had not operated, and the head man said that he should have been warned of their coming, as they might have been mistaken for the police and shot. After that every courtesy was shown, and my colleague and his companion were driven to the rubber factory in a very old bus.

These stories are not technical material, but I quote them to under-line that loss adjusting in certain parts of the world is very different from work at home: the danger of being shot is not really regarded as an occupational hazard by loss adjusters in this country. A colleague of mine based in Latin America was threatened by the insured with a gun, and very nearly shot, when what appeared to be an ordinary robbery of gold bullion emerged as a most involved affair of international smuggling. And representatives in Indonesia have on several occasions been fired upon when travelling to tea and rubber estates following bandit raids. There the situation remains just as bad as it was in Burma several years ago, although from different causes. The danger is such that it is not safe to travel out of the main towns, and police and military protection is unobtainable. Consequently it is very difficult to investigate claims there; but equally it is almost impossible for the agricultural estates to be kept working. I believe that very little insurance is now written on country risks in Indonesia, which at least saves the loss adjuster from having to consider any more whether claims situations there constitute insurable riots or not. Wherever they occur, riots seldom seem to follow exactly the conception of a riot contained in the standard wording; and even though the wording was revised a few years ago, matters do not seem to be much easier.

The Assam fire, and the Burmese fires which I have referred to, all followed a pattern which becomes very familiar in the tropics. A timber building thoroughly dried out by the heat, with a corrugated iron roof. A fire pump and hoses, but a very restricted water supply, or even no water at all. A great deal of confusion, and general unpreparedness. These conditions spell a total loss, and that is almost invariably what occurs.

In the UK timber is regarded most unfavourably by insurers as a principal building material, but in the tropics (other than in desert countries, where it does not exist locally in any quantity) it is the material used more than any other. And galvanised corrugated iron, or zinc, as it is sometimes called, is the foremost roofing material in the world. There is a great deal to be said for both of them. They are cheap, easily transported, and easily worked by the semi-skilled labour that is probably all that is available. In warmer climates than ours they are durable, but readily repaired when the iron has rusted or the timber has been affected by insects. They withstand earthquakes better than bricks and concrete, the overseas standard of which is not universally high. In many areas they are more congenial to live in.

Obviously a wooden building exhibits a much greater fire danger than a concrete one. But where whole communities live and work amongst timber a certain discipline concerning fire precautions grows

142

up, and very great care is taken, in rather the same way as in the Australian bush, where it is a *social* offence to throw away a match during the dry season; it must be returned to the matchbox. However, when a timber building does catch fire it is not easy to put the fire out; and the hotter and drier the climate, the easier it becomes to start the fire and the more quickly it will burn. For instance, during the summer months in the Persian Gulf it is not difficult to set fire to a sizeable piece of rough-sawn wood with just one match. High temperatures tend to associate with small water supplies for extinguishment, and so the hazard grows. Comparatively, in a dry atmosphere and continuous day temperatures of around 100°F., fire will travel through a wooden building at three times the rate it would in this country, so that a far greater degree of damage is done in the same time.

Asbestos-cement sheeting is also used a great deal in walls and roofs, but is less popular in the remoter areas because it does not travel well. From the fire aspect its disadvantage is that it will expand like a sail between the nails that hold it and finally crack up, allowing draughts to form and the flames to escape. Corrugated iron will hold flames behind it so long as the structural timber resists. Asbestos disintegrates, and when it does so there is always a series of loud reports. Quite often one hears stories of quite innocent insured who must have kept supplies of ammunition in buildings containing asbestos, or must have set the fire with a series of explosions. The bending of this material is sometimes quite dramatic in fire conditions. I remember seeing the asbestos wall of a village hall in Victoria where the six-foot sheets had pulled out all the four-inch nails by which they were secured in the middle before finally contracting back into place.

Corrugated aluminium is also coming into fashion, particularly in conjunction with prefabricated steel structural members. This material tends to melt and burn at relatively low temperatures, leading to draughts, escapes of flame, and so on.

Overseas fire brigades vary tremendously in equipment and efficiency, and it is not really possible to generalize. Belize in British Honduras possesses three La France engines built in 1919, with a top speed of 10 m.p.h.; but there is a modern Dennis appliance as well. Whatever the efficiency of a brigade may be, it can be no faster in reaching a fire than the speed of the telephone service permits, and in underwriting this is sometimes a point which should be investigated. In some Middle Eastern countries and elsewhere nothing happens when one tries to telephone, and it is usually quicker to run than telephone. In certain places (the Persian Gulf and parts of the Caribbean, for example) fresh water is extremely short, and sea water is used for extinguishment. When salt water is directed on to a fire involving metals, textiles, chemicals, and so on a very substantial degree of damage is caused, and in general what is not destroyed by the fire is rendered a total loss by the water. Even if the damaged property is immediately washed in fresh water, oil, petrol, or carbon tetrachloride it is extremely difficult to remove all traces of salt, which will collect moisture from the air, so that rusting or decomposition continues.

The effects of salt water were seen very clearly in Belize after the 1961 hurricane. The hurricane was accompanied by a twelve-foot tidal wave, and as the town lies only one foot above sea level the water swept right through the town and then became mixed with the acid mud of the mangrove swamp behind the town. Belize possesses a rather rudimentary sewage system by which waste products flow down open sewers into the central river. I understand that the true bottom of the river has never been plumbed. Winds of 200 m.p.h. mixed the salt water, the mud from the mangroves, and the other materials from the bottom of the sewers and the river, but it was only the water that flowed away. What remained of the town was therefore coated with up to two feet of thick black matter with a strong salt and some acid content.

This case will be memorable to the loss adjusters concerned for the unprecedented hardships it caused to the local population, many of whom lost everything. Over one-half of the houses were destroyed or rendered uninhabitable in any sense; and in the beginning there were no food supplies or other supplies of any kind, no transport, no electricity, no telephones, and only such water as could be collected from rainwater butts. Everywhere there was the thick filthy mud, and in many places the smell of bodies under the debris. Belize cannot be quickly forgotten. Although the hurricane winds were responsible for blowing over buildings and destroying the electricity and telephone networks it was the water and mud that created most of the damage. The population was too shocked to start clearing up as early as would otherwise have been possible, and the water and mud lay around for some time, corroding almost everything with which it came into contact. Rolls of textiles, clothing, shoes, and so on disintegrated as soon as they were touched. Furniture fell into its component parts. Body panels on cars rusted through in a matter of days. This was the first occasion on which I learned that cars floated. Many travelled half a mile. One prominent businessman had just

144

bought a new Rover and had the unhappy experience of seeing it float out of his garage and across the road into the vacant garage of a bank manager opposite. After that it floated back again, and when the water receded it was parked precisely where it had been left, completely undamaged except by the water. There were many other unusual features associated with this hurricane: a piano which was blown fifty yards, and a number of closed and locked cars which had dead fish in them. The last seems to have no acceptable explanation at all.

Now for fraudulent fire claims. I do not think it would be unfair to say that the incidence of such claims experienced in overseas fire departments is far greater than in home departments, and it is an unfortunate fact that in certain places commercial morality is not valued very highly. In the United Kingdom we have the full weight of an efficient police force and forensic laboratories of every kind, but such facilities are not available universally. With wooden buildings overseas the intended total loss so often occurs, and the flames destroy all evidence of their origin. These fires seem always to occur in the early hours of the morning, when nobody is around to witness anything or to call the brigade. Local people are shy of the loss adjuster and the police (in very few countries do the police enjoy the confidence and public support that they receive here) and by the time the adjuster reaches the scene the whole premises have probably been overrun by looters. These factors do not make matters easy.

The nearer one gets to the sun the greater the number of people who come forward or write anonymous letters to say that the fire was set for the insurance money. This happens with such regularity that it is dangerous to look at a fire suspiciously for this reason alone. But all fire loss adjusters pride themselves that they possess an instinct to detect a fraudulent fire almost immediately, and I believe this instinct exists, although I cannot define it.

In a case of suspected arson the question to be answered is, how would the insured benefit? If there is no benefit then almost certainly there is no arson. But if evidence can be found of substantial over-insurance, or out-of-date stock, or recent heavy movements of stock out of the premises, or something of that nature, very careful enquiries have to be made. It is extremely difficult at home to establish arson, and outside Europe, North America, and Australasia it is even more difficult. Everywhere courts are reluctant to convict on circumstantial evidence alone, and if some possibility exists that the fire could have arisen by other means then a dismissal is to be expected. In this context we all hear so frequently of the 'electrical fault', which in practice is impossible to prove or disprove. So the insurer is left to explore the possibility of avoiding liability on a technicality; but even if such a possibility exists, a number of countries have legislation which almost totally discounts misrepresentation and non-disclosure, whilst in others a foreign insurer can hardly hope to succeed at arbitration or litigation against a national. This brings another case to mind, a fire in a large factory which was heavily over-insured by a man nearly bankrupt who was seen running amongst the flames, and was afterwards found to have petrol on his clothing, whilst more petrol in containers of every kind was found in the undamaged sections of the premises. This was an almost textbook situation, but the insurers had to pay. The reason is probably best explained by allusion. Large premises tend to suggest owners prominent in local affairs, and, if they are so inclined, in local politics also. In places where official appointments are made politically it is possible to find that the chief justice is the brother of the owner of the large premises, and the chief of police his best friend. Insurers just cannot hope to succeed in this sort of situation, for if they do not pay they stand to forfeit their underwriting deposits.

Not infrequently the loss adjuster will be offered a bribe. This, of course, is very reprehensible, but it is only fair to consider the problem in its local context, for business standards abroad are not always the same as those at home; and very probably the insured concerned will be doing no more than conducting a commercial transaction in the way in which such affairs are conducted locally. On such factors must depend whether the offer is declined politely or in some other manner. There are people who will go to any lengths to acquire insurance money. I recall the case of another colleague of mine who was instructed to decline liability on a fraudulent fire, whereupon the insured laid 'evidence' with the police that the adjuster had not only accepted bribes but had also stolen large quantities of salvage and tampered with the evidence of the fire. In reality it was the police who had been bribed, and it was their evidence that was bought. The whole matter went before the criminal courts, but it was many worrying months before an acquittal was obtained; and it was also a very costly business.

The standard of policies written overseas, often by agents of British insurers, is not always high. There has often been little attempt to understand even the simplest principles of insurance, and covers are sometimes issued that are not in the least what was intended. They may even be meaningless. As usual, the insured never studies his policy, and the trouble does not come to light until there has been a loss. Buildings are wrongly described, there are often muddles over names, addresses, bases of valuation, and insured perils. I remember that one insurance covering a factory whose purpose was to boil fats and oils into soap was subject to a warranty that 'no boiling process be carried on'. Where a British insurer or his agent has been guilty of these mistakes I have always found the local companies to be very quick in trying to capitalize on them, and in this respect the criticism is a serious one. Mistakes create settlement delays, and the British insurer cannot receive high regard locally when a local insurer has paid out his proportion six weeks earlier on the same fire.

The Thole Produce Yard fire in Karachi in 1949 produced the greatest complexity of covers that I have experienced. It was a cotton fire totalling about £1 million, and was the one which I believe finally demonstrated that a full-pressed bale of cotton *could* be totally consumed. It also produced a most complicated apportionment. Merchants insured their cotton in the yard, and one policy, say, would cover cotton at four separate locations in separate amounts. Another policy would insure locations one and three whilst another insurance would cover locations one, two, and four. Then yet another policy would be produced for locations one and four, plus a general floater covering stocks anywhere in the yard, a second floater covering the insured and a bank jointly, and a third floater insuring stocks in which the merchant was jointly interested with his brother. Then the brother would have some policies as well; and although there are ways of performing the figurework in this kind of situation (and it is not for the loss adjuster to criticize the policies before him) we often felt that matters could have been made simpler for everybody, not least the insured. In the same vein, a merchant in Malta held over thirty policies on stock, all at the same premises and with the same office. Some of them went back fifty years. When his stock value went up he took out another policy; when it decreased he found an insurance for approximately the amount involved and cancelled it. His brokers had never told him about declaration insurances. Again, it is not really for the loss adjuster to comment, but having estimated the loss in a case like this he can be tempted to estimate the number of premium calculations that would have been made over fifty years.

In Belize we encountered a most extraordinary situation over two policies. This was no fault of the insurers. A man owned a house, insured it, leased it to a tenant, and then died. The tenant did not like the house, so he knocked it down and built another on the site and insured that. Both policies were running when the house was badly damaged by the hurricane. I believe the offices concerned came to an amicable arrangement over the matter, but I have never been sure of the text-book answer to this problem.

After the Thole Yard fire just mentioned arrangements were made with two local merchants for the handling and reconditioning of the salvage, and an enormous operation was finally concluded with very satisfactory salvage return. Karachi is a cotton town, and sufficient labour and machinery were readily available. Any other commodity would have produced difficulty. Generally speaking, there are few facilities overseas for handling, drying, and treating salvage; and of course, there are few salvage corps. In small communities it is also most difficult to dispose of salvage at a satisfactory price, if at all. Consequently an overseas fire which is not a total loss must tend to produce a greater percentage of loss than an equivalent one in the UK.

Of recent years there seems to have been a considerable growth in the underwriting of contractors' all-risks and third-party business overseas. Claims under this type of insurance, be it home or overseas, represent a subject in themselves, and I can do no more than touch upon it here. Wordings appear to be constantly on the move, yet the contractors continue to create claims situations that do not appear quite to fit the wordings. They have 'accidents' that are not quite accidents; they sustain 'losses' that may or may not be losses, depending upon how the problem is viewed. And there is the ever-present difficulty in storm, flood, and malicious damage cases of fixing the *number* of losses to enable the excess figure to be established. However, these matters are common to both home and overseas policies, and indeed the types of claim encountered overseas are no different from the ones at home. The pattern of claims becomes different outside the industrialized countries of the world, however, because of the quality of the labour available to the contractor on the site, and, in mechanical contracts, the quality of the staff and labour who are in charge during the maintenance period. One so often encounters men driving Euclids whose experience up to six months before was restricted to bicycles – and inevitably the Euclid is overturned, or left at the top of a hill with the brakes off, or driven into the river. Mechanics search for petrol leaks with lighted matches. Turbine drivers are fully instructed in lubrication, but they forget, and bearings run dry. None of these causes is unknown at home, but a very much greater incidence is seen in the underdeveloped countries. And there are more liability claims springing from the same root cause – vehicles knocking people over, spanners dropped on people's heads, and so on. It is just not possible to preach safety to everybody. I remember that in Bombay it was the custom of the port workers to sleep after lunch, and the favoured place was under a railway truck with their heads on the railway lines. Shunting resumed after lunch, and they were decapitated with distressing frequency.

When an injury involving a third party occurs in certain countries of the Middle East it is the custom for everybody who might have been responsible to be put in prison at once. They stay there until bailed out for a sum roughly equivalent to the potential damages, but automatically a case remains pending which may be heard in three, four, or five years. If the case is against a foreign national or foreign firm neither has any great prospect of success, and meanwhile a large sum of money remains idle and the individuals concerned have restrictions imposed upon them; for example, their passports and driving licences may be confiscated. But the matter can be closed if the claimant or his beneficiary writes to the court requesting this. These letters obviously possess a market price, dependent not so much on liability or damages as on the inconvenience that will be suffered by the defendant, and the lawyers are very well aware of this. The defendant just has to buy himself out of an impossible situation, and the price can be very high indeed.

Many projects have been carried out by British, European, and United States contractors in countries newly independent, and in underdeveloped countries. These schemes are usually tied to foreign aid of some kind, and the donor nations take care that their money is carefully spent by first ensuring that the project is well founded, and by supplying technical aid on site. Or they may be contracts involving Western defence. Contracts of this kind tend to show far less risk to the insurer than ones in which new government buildings, hotels, palaces, and other prestige structures are being erected by local contractors in the newly emerging nations, designed and supervised by local architects. These buildings usually defy the local conventions, and often all conventions, and almost inevitably there is trouble which will involve insurers. Expansions and stresses are wrongly calculated, or perhaps the contractor decides to economize on the cement content of his concrete. There are exclusions to protect the insurer in this sort of situation, but they are not infrequently deleted, or for various reasons may be difficult to prove. In contracting, experimentation and inexperience are always expensive.

149

Now for burglary claims. Of course this type of cover is not freely issued everywhere, because of the high incidence of losses, or because of the difficulty of establishing the amount of any individual loss. At home, in trade risks, it is possible to calculate pre-loss and post-loss stock figures, and the difference has been stolen. Or at least there is some prima facie evidence of the amount involved. But the adjusting of the loss is not so easy in communities where no books are kept; or where three different sets of books are kept – one for the fiscal authorities, one for the sleeping partner, and one actual, with yet another set written up for the purposes of the claim. This often happens, and it is always so obvious: new books, written in the same hand, with the same bottle of ink, purporting to show figures extending over three years. Inflated claims are to be expected, and although difficulties of the same kind are experienced in fire cases, with a fire there is at least something to see. To some extent assistance can be obtained from tax returns, if they exist. But so many taxation authorities experience exactly the same kind of difficulties, and have no alternative but to do a deal with the trader without specific reference to the value of his stock. For example, many emigrant Chinese and Syrian traders about the world keep their books in Chinese or Arabic, which is quite unintelligible to the local authorities.

There have been a few famous exceptions, but burglaries and robberies planned and executed with military precision and enormous skill seldom seem to occur outside Europe and North America. I know a number of members of the criminal community in London, and there is no doubt that if their talents had been directed to other channels several of them would occupy very high positions. Perhaps these people do not exist except in Europe and North America. Outside these areas the burglary seems to be something of a casual affair, in which the thief breaks in and is thankful for anything he can find. The actual entry is often simplified in the tropics by the light construction of the building, with windows permanently open, or louvres in place of windows. Or there may be an armed hold-up of the wages car on a lonely road. However, master planning and organization are not often encountered, and special skills in locks and safeblowing are not often seen.

Some local specialities exist. In Jamaica a long pole with a hook at the end is pushed through the open bedroom window at night and jacket and trousers fished off the back of a chair, together with the contents of the pockets. In Africa burglars strip near-naked and grease themselves so that they are impossible to hold if apprehended.

In the East children are pushed through very small openings and unlock buildings from the inside. In all these countries it is the custom to employ night watchmen, but they seem to be of very little value beyond creating a general deterrent. In West Africa, for instance, they come on duty carrying their bedding rolls. At the time of the loss these watchmen will be either off the premises conversing with other watchmen, or asleep. Often they are armed, but sometimes this is of little help either. I remember the case of an Indian watchman who had been in the army and was very smart indeed. He guarded an hotel, and had a twelve-bore shotgun and a bandolier of cartridges which he kept in immaculate condition. It was only after the bandits had escaped that the discovery was made that for five years the watchman had polished his cartridge caps daily with metal polish, so that inevitably a certain dampness had penetrated inside.

Infidelity claims and bank frauds are also encountered far more abroad than at home. The Middle East comes principally to mind, which is perhaps not altogether surprising when cashiers handling tens of thousands of pounds a day are found to earn the equivalent of ninety shillings a week. Often the culprit will work for an absentee employer, whilst in banks the visits of the inspectors will probably be infrequent because of the shortage of inspecting staff or the remoteness of the branch. Irregularities in bank cases have been known to go on for years, involving enormous sums of money. Sometimes the culprit is caught, but more often he disappears at the time of discovery and cannot be found; or alternatively jumps his bail. By this time the money is well spread round the family and recovery is very difficult.

It is no more possible to generalize about the efficiency of overseas police forces than it is about fire brigades. Most appear to be overworked and understaffed, and the majority, I think, could not claim the 40–50 per cent of solved crime achieved by the police at home. Where national characteristics suggest a certain indolence the police are probably indolent also, and it is necessary to offer some material encouragement if results are to be achieved. And if results are achieved, gratitude in a material form is looked for afterwards. This is entirely customary in some of the South American republics, and I remember one senior officer who at the successful conclusion of a case prepared for insurers' consideration a list of requirements which included two Chevrolets (different models) and a case of guns. Major crime is solved on information, and this is what had happened in this case. The officer had not over-exerted himself, but he considered he was entitled to about £3000 in kind; and most certainly he had to receive something if any results were to be achieved in future cases.

Another type of crime which seems to be increasing is that involving the theft of high-value air sendings – diamonds, banknotes, gold, and so on. Most are sent by registered mail, but be they mail or freight, the solution of the crime is always an extremely difficult matter. In fairness to the airlines, however, it must be said that the losses represent only a minute proportion of the total traffic, which is the reason why the diamond trade, the banks, and others have come to rely on this means of conveyance. Figures are better left unpublicized, but for London Airport alone the weekly value handled is enormous.

It only takes ten seconds to violate a mailbag and remove some of the contents. If the bag carries a red tag on the label it is a registered bag and will have something of value in it. The place of origin of the bag will probably be printed on it, its destination on the label. Thus a Johannesburg/London registered bag will almost certainly have diamonds in it somewhere, and if there is any doubt about packages the name and address of the consignee will give every help. Equally, banknotes pack into parcels with a limited number of sizes, and the parcel is almost always addressed to a bank. So the selected package is stolen from the bag, and the aircraft starts or continues its journey. Even if discovery is made immediately after landing at the final destination there is no indication where the loss occurred – it might be there or at any route point over, say, eight countries and ten thousand miles. But the refinement is to slide up the string around the neck of the bag, make a cut in the neck below the string, remove the package, and slide the string down again. The cut then becomes concealed in the folds at the neck of the bag, and discovery of the violation cannot be made until the bag is emptied. This introduces even more possibilities into the location of the crime. It usually *can* be solved in the end, even if proof is not possible; but whether or not there is a recovery depends on other factors.

In this paper I have tried to bring out the fundamental importance of flexibility in loss adjusting overseas and to demonstrate that, whilst doing in Rome what the Romans do may not always be morally justified, it is nevertheless both politic and necessary to respect their customs if one wishes to do business with them. I would also say that whilst certain places and peoples have been mentioned in certain contexts and my comments may remain relevant for many years –

it would seem that the leopard does not often change his spots – societies and local conditions do change with consequent effect on loss adjusting considerations.

25 February 1963

Appendix II

Trundle, Heap and Baker

THE MERGER of Toplis and Harding with Trundle, Heap and Baker on 1 July 1987 created one of the largest loss adjusting firms in the world. Trundle, Heap and Baker originated in a firm that was highly regarded in the early years of the century, William Owen and Company. William Owen had been born in Caernarvon, and was the brother of E. Roger Owen, a distinguished General Manager of the Commercial Union Assurance Co. William Owen had come to London and become employed by one of the most significant assessing companies of the time, I. E. Rouch & Co. In 1907, representing I. E. Rouch, William Owen was one of the founder-members of the Insurance Institute of London.

Edwin Francis Trundle joined Owen's firm soon after the 1914–18 War. He was Australian: his father was the Commercial Union's manager at Brisbane, and young Edwin had gone into his father's office as a clerk. Then in 1914, at the age of 25, he had volunteered like so many young Australians of his generation to fight for the 'home country'; he was in the first contingent of Australian troops to arrive in Europe. He served through the war, and ended as a Captain. Visiting London before going home, he called into the Commercial Union office and asked Roger Owen whether he could spend a month with one of the company's assessors, to gain experience in handling claims. Roger Owen passed him on to his brother William.

Perhaps because he was not 'local', he was asked to deal with one of the most sensitive claims on the books. It was a claim for £100,000 made by Sir Jeremiah Colman, then Chairman of the Commercial Union. E. F. Trundle handled it so effectively that William Owen asked him to remain in London, and offered him a partnership, which he accepted. He did not see Australia again for 30 years. It was decided to open an office in Liverpool (still a wealthy commercial centre, and the home of the Cunard transatlantic liners), and Trundle

154

moved to Liverpool to take charge of that branch of William Owen and Company, first in Victoria Street and then in Exchange Street East. Once that office was working well, Trundle returned to London headquarters in Queen Victoria Street.

He then spent a period travelling extensively dealing with major losses around the world. He was particularly fond of two stories from those days. In South America he was pursuing a claim when he received an anonymous letter threatening that he would have a knife thrust into him if he did not back off. He did not, but kept the letter and had it framed on his office wall in the London office, which had moved to Walbrook. On another occasion, Lloyd's underwriters asked him to go to the United States, where the number of insurances for tornado damage seemed to have increased to a startling degree. He soon established that many proposals had been accepted almost minutes before the tornado struck, and his evidence greatly helped the insurance market.

When Trundle returned to London, the Liverpool office was taken over by John Simpson Foulkes DSO. He too had an association with the Commercial Union since his father had been a branch manager. J. S. Foulkes had ended the 1914–18 War as a Major, and had joined William Owen in charge of the Liverpool office at 30 Exchange Street East when Owen returned to London. In 1930 William Owen died. For a time, his former partners kept the business going under his name. Then on 1 June 1933 a new firm, Trundle, Foulkes and Co. was constituted with offices in London (at Worcester House, 7/8 Walbrook) and Liverpool. Joining the old partners of Edwin Trundle and John Foulkes were two new partners: Sidney E. Arber (who came from Toplis and Harding) and Frederick E. Stacy. Among the former staff of Owens who translated to the new firm were several characters: one was Mr Kitchenside, a building surveyor, who was one of the organizers of the National Brass Band Festival and spent his winter Saturday afternoons conducting the Arsenal Football Club Band – several of his staff colleagues became keen Arsenal supporters on complimentary tickets.

In 1934 David Victor Diamond joined the staff from the Eagle Star Insurance Company to open an Accident Department in London. The largest case he handled was in fact on Merseyside, when in 1939 a lift at Hamilton Square Station on the Mersey (underground) Railway crashed to the bottom of the lift shaft during the evening rush hour. More than 80 passengers suffered injuries, many severe. All the claims were settled by 'Di' without litigation, for a total of slightly over £80,000.

The 1939–45 war made great difficulties for the firm, particularly in London. In both London and Liverpool, much of the work consisted of assessing war damage for the Board of Trade. One member of the staff, H. F. Crohn, recalled that

> Work . . . was strenuous and trying both physically and mentally. Ordinary insurance losses by fire, burglary, storm etc. continued and as soon as bombing commenced the War Damage Department of the Board of Trade was organized and claims came in by the hundred. Work was rendered difficult in the extreme, and dangerous. Many times the adjuster would have to tiptoe warily along roads where access was barred to ordinary traffic on account of unexploded bombs. It was also necessary to go near partly wrecked buildings wondering whether a wall would remain standing for the time it took to get past it. Government regulations and restrictions were severe and difficult to memorize and observe and to make matters worse, claimants were in many cases shocked and unnerved which made them unreasonable and more than ordinarily difficult to deal with.
>
> Then, having done a hard day's work the weary adjuster would grope his way home in the blackout and probably spend an uncomfortable evening sitting in a damp and cold air raid shelter writing reports by the light of a candle or dim paraffin lamp.

The work of the London office was transferred to Mr Trundle's home at Cheam, Surrey, and Walbrook kept as a City base. In May 1941 the Walbrook office was destroyed by a bomb and the City staff worked for a time from Sidney Arber's home in East Finchley. From 1942, however, there was a return to the City, and rooms were taken at 23 Old Jewry. In 1943 Sidney Arber died, and the Finchley office was closed. In June 1944 a flying bomb landed in Old Jewry, hitting the office of the Public Trustee and driving Trundle, Foulkes and Co. temporarily to the Commercial Union headquarters in Cornhill, before an office was found at 99/100 Cheapside, and later at 80 Coleman Street. (This was just four months before a V1 rocket landed in Old Jewry, destroying the offices of Toplis and Harding.)

With the ending of war in 1945 there was no decrease in work, largely due to backlogs in war damage claims, and also the widening of policy cover. The strain of the war years had its casualties: John Foulkes died in Liverpool in 1946, aged 56. His son Eric Foulkes had joined his regiment at the outbreak of war, sailed for the Far East, was captured by the Japanese, and spent the war in a prison camp. On his return to England he worked as a quantity surveyor while qualifying as a Chartered Surveyor, then as an Associate of the Chartered Insurance Institute and finally as a Fellow of the Association of Loss

Adjusters. In 1949 he married Jeanne, the only daughter of Sidney Arber; he rejoined the 'family firm' in 1953 and became a partner in 1958.

On the death of D. V. Diamond in 1955 the Accident Department was closed, and the business taken over by his assistants as Doman, Ground and Co. Edwin Francis Trundle died on 9 September 1955, at the age of 65. He had been instrumental in founding the Association of Fire Loss Adjusters, of which he was President in 1950. (His partner, A. T. Ridley, was to be in 1962 first President of its successor body, the Chartered Institute of Loss Adjusters.) E. F. Trundle had been a notable figure in the profession, and had represented all the leading insurance offices and Lloyd's underwriters. A. B. Carter and A. T. Ridley were left as Senior Partners of Trundle, Foulkes and Co.

In 1960 A. B. Carter dealt with a record fire loss at the Rolls Royce works at Mount Sorrell, Leicestershire, which was agreed after considerable work, at just under two and a quarter million pounds. Assisting him was R. S. Tuff, who had joined the staff a few years earlier from the insurance department of the Central Electricity Board, and subsequently became a partner. This was to be a period of expansion for the firm. In the early sixties branch offices were opened in South Wales and Cardiff, and an informal working relationship was agreed with A. Baker and Co. of Bristol, with offices in Plymouth, Exeter and Cheltenham. In the North West, offices were opened in Lancaster and Preston.

From 1966 these and other informal agreements were put on a business footing. The firm of Trundle, Foulkes and Co. was wound up and replaced by Trundle, Heap and Baker, representing a merger between Trundles and W. Graham Heap and Co. of Manchester, Liverpool and Preston, and A. Baker and Co. of Bristol and the West Country. This was to lead to a prosperous development lasting over the next twenty years.

In 1987 the head office of Trundle, Heap and Baker was in Dominion House, Bartholomew Close, in the City. There were 27 offices throughout the country, eight partners and 180 staff. In principle, the business was that of chartered loss adjusting within Britain; though some international business was undertaken, this derived in all cases from within the home business. On the agreement to merge with Toplis and Harding, a new firm was initially created on 1 July 1987 – Toplis, Trundle Limited. Of the original partners, five remained: J. R. Ellwood, A. G. Rackstraw, M. W. France, D. B. Clement and D. H. Crosbie. In 1989 the name of 'Toplis, Trundle Ltd' was dropped and the business became – as Toplis UK – a division of the Toplis and Harding Group, with 52 offices and a staff of 400.

Wm. Elmslie & Son

THE NAME of Elmslie was well known in the City of London in the eighteenth century. An Elmslie was a Lloyd's underwriter and he appears as a defendant underwriter in two law reports of the 1790s. But it was in 1843 that William Elmslie began practising as an average adjuster. He was elected an Annual Subscriber to Lloyd's in 1848, and in 1869 became a founding member of the Association of Average Adjusters (AAA). When he took his elder son into partnership in 1871 the name of the firm became Wm. Elmslie & Son.

At that time the traditional work of the average adjuster was the preparation of hull and cargo statements. In 1878 a second son, Kenward Wallace Elmslie, joined the partnership. He soon proved to be an extremely energetic and effective young man (he had already worked his way round the world on a windjammer, so he could talk to sea-captains as well as ship-owners on their own terms). He was elected an Annual Subscriber to Lloyd's in 1880, the year that his father died.

Soon afterwards he was consulted by Lord Bearstead of M. Samuel & Co. about a claim on Japanese matches. They got on well together, and when Samuel & Co. began to run ships, Wm. Elmslie & Son was retained to deal with all insurance claims of the company that, as it grew, became Shell Transport and Trading Co. Ltd. The Shell Group of companies remains the most valued and important single client of Wm. Elmslie & Son. Meanwhile K. W. Elmslie was becoming active in other areas, as Chairman of the Association of Average Adjusters in 1888, and one of the first Associates of Lloyd's when that title was introduced in 1893. He became involved with many aspects of insurance internationally, and was one of the prime movers in the successful introduction of codes of practice for average adjusters in the 1890s, and a Vice-President of the International Law Association from 1913.

In 1914 his elder son 'Keno' was killed in one of the early battles of the 1914–18 War, as a Lieutenant in the 4th Royal Irish Dragoon Guards. It may have been this that impelled K. W. Elmslie to take on a heavy load of government work during that war, giving his services to advise several Royal Commissions on matters concerning cargoes and shipping, and preparing adjustments for the Foreign Office.

Soon after the war, in 1920, his second son Gordon Forbes Elmslie was taken into partnership. They worked in harness for nearly a decade, until K. W. Elmslie died at the end of 1929. He was remembered for his keen sense of humour, and his generosity to many good causes, particularly Dr Barnardo's Homes (one of his sisters had married Dr Barnardo). It no doubt reflects on K. W. Elmslie's ability to judge men, and his fairness as an employer, that six young men he recruited between 1916 and 1921 (three of them from the same school at Greenwich) stayed with the firm for a total of 299 years – the last, F. W. Shepperd, died while still in the firm's employment in 1983. In 1926 K. W. Elmslie also introduced the first non-family partner to the firm, Philip Robinson Bennett.

Gordon Forbes Elmslie was senior partner from 1929: like most City men of the time, he maintained standards of dress that were becoming old-fashioned: he would customarily appear in an 'Anthony Eden' hat and spats. His son K. G. Elmslie, after taking a first in law at Cambridge, briefly joined the firm, but then became a district officer in the Colonial Service in Africa before returning to the City, eventually to become senior partner of the solicitors Richards Butler. G. F. Elmslie was Chairman of the AAA in 1940, and his partner P. R. Bennett in 1943 (Bennett's son W. P. F. 'Bill' Bennett was to hold the same office in 1980).

Following G. F. Elmslie's death in 1955, P. R. Bennett became senior partner, joined in 1958 by H. E. W. Bowyer (who left the firm in 1981) and in 1959 by W. P. F. Bennett. There followed a period of expansion. In 1968 WES bought the business of W. R. M. Stevens in Hong Kong upon Mr Stevens' retirement, and formed Stevens Elmslie & Co. (SECO). In 1969 N. W. Stevens, son of W. R. M., passed his AAA examinations and became a partner in SECO. In 1971 SECO opened an office in Taipei and later in Manila and Singapore. (In 1986 the partners of Wm. Elmslie & Son sold their interest in SECO to NWS.)

In 1971 William Elmslie & Son acquired the business of Bennett & Co., which had been formed in 1937 by Edward Osborne Bennett, a member of the AAA and father of the principal of the firm at this time, Horace S. Bennett (and also, incidentally, first cousin of 'Bill' Bennett who had succeeded his father as senior partner of Wm.

Elmslie & Son in 1969). It happened that the founder of Bennett & Co. had died in 1943 before his son had qualified; his son Horace S. Bennett determined to keep the family business going, but never did sit his examinations and qualify. Thus when Wm. Elmslie & Son acquired the firm in 1971, the partners were precluded by the AAA rules from practising in partnership with H. S. Bennett, who acted for many years only as a consultant to Wm. Elmslie & Son.

The firm's work had for many years involved, with other business, acting as marine claims advisers to the marine side of Shell. Indeed, from 1924–62 Wm. Elmslie & Son occupied offices in the Shell building at 29 Great St Helens Place. In 1939–40 Shell moved its marine staff briefly down to Plymouth, Elmslies went too. When Shell built its new headquarters by Waterloo Bridge in 1962, the firm had a suite of rooms in the Shell Centre. During the 1970s the nature of the firm's work in the oil industry expanded beyond this valued association. Principally due to the discovery of oil and gas in the North Sea, Wm. Elmslie & Son became involved in some energy adjusting and a considerable amount of claims advising during both the development and production stages of off-shore fields, first in the North Sea and subsequently worldwide. This expansion was helped by the firm's knowledge of the oil industry through its work for Shell, but the new claims came mostly from oil companies other than Shell.

In 1976 the firm started to give claims advice, both marine and non-marine, to Occidental Petroleum (Oxy). The amount of work increased rapidly and successfully. In 1982 the firm's first office was opened in the USA, in Los Angeles, at the specific request of Oxy whose corporate headquarters was there. Subsequently another office was opened in Rhode Island. Initially the work consisted of co-ordinating and processing both marine and non-marine claims world-wide for the Oxy Group. Later a team of risk engineers was employed to survey Oxy marine and non-marine facilities worldwide.

In the early 1980s an increasing amount of energy adjusting was being obtained in Canada. Wm. Elmslie & Son opened an office in Calgary, the oil capital. In 1983 the firm acquired a minority interest in the Liverpool practice of Danson Finlason Loftus & May (Danson) (see below). The whole of Danson equity was acquired by Elmslies in 1988. In 1989 there was a further acquisition when the sole partner in A. H. May & Son, the Glasgow firm of Average Adjusters, retired and his business was acquired by Toplis Elmslie Marine.

Danson Finlason Loftus & May

This firm was formally an amalgamation of three old-established and respected partnerships in Liverpool: F. C. Danson & Co., A. M. & W. Finlason, and Henry Loftus and Partners. There was also an association with A. H. May & Son of Glasgow.

F. C. Danson & Co. was founded by Francis Danson, whose father J. T. Danson was a journalist (and assistant to Charles Dickens), farmer, barrister, and writer of the largest marine account of the day as underwriter of the Thames and Mersey Marine. The young Danson was apprenticed to Richard Lowndes, and then boldly set up business in 1879 in the same building in Liverpool. In 1902 the White Star Line and other shipping was bought by J. Pierpont Morgan, and as a consequence Danson opened an office in London, which eventually joined Wm. Elmslie & son at 9 St Helens Place.

A. M. & W. Finlason was founded by A. M. Finlason who trained with Walter Lowndes and started his own business in Liverpool in 1906. Henry Loftus and Partners was created in Liverpool in 1899 by Henry Loftus who broke with his family firm of H. M. Loftus & Sons. Control of the firm passed to A. M. & W. Finlason in 1932. A. H. May & Son was founded by A. H. May, who after working as a clerk at Lloyd's became secretary of the Union Marine Insurance Co. in Liverpool, and then moved to Glasgow in the average adjusting partnership of D. W. MacKechnie. From 1911 the firm was A. H. May & Son, and became associated with F. C. Danson & Co. in 1946.

Dates
A Chronology of Toplis and Harding

1790   *James Toplis* begins work in the City of London

1798   Toplis becomes Freeman of the Upholders' Company

c.1809   Moves business to 30 St Paul's Churchyard

1810   Fire destroys premises

1811   Toplis appointed Surveyor of Stock to the Sun Fire Office
       Moves business to 22 St Paul's Churchyard

1813   Toplis takes John Woolfitt as partner, and the firm becomes *Toplis and Woolfitt*.

1820   Woolfitt leaves to start his own business, and the firm becomes *Toplis and Co.*

1824   Toplis auctions fire salvage for the Exchange, Sun and West of England Fire Offices

1826   James Toplis jun. becomes Freeman of the Upholders' Company
       Business becomes *Toplis and Son*

1836   James Toplis sen. becomes Warden of the Upholders' Company

1841   Auctions St Bartholomew's church, Royal Exchange

1843   Assessor for the Sun Office after the Luton Hoo fire

1844   William Daniel Harding joins the firm
       Business becomes *Toplis, Son and Harding*

1848   James Toplis auctions contents of Hexton House, Herts

1857   W. D. Harding becomes a partner

1861   Auctions salvage after Horseleydown fire for the Sun, Phoenix and Royal Exchange offices

1867   Business becomes *Toplis and Harding*

1885   W. D. Harding succeeded by his sons William Daniel Harding jun. and Edward Ernest Harding

c.1880   Edward Ernest Harding becomes senior partner

1890   Moves business to 80 St Paul's Churchyard

1895   Graham Harding (son of E. E. Harding) joins firm

1910 Graham Harding becomes senior partner on death of E. E. Harding. Moves business to Cannon Street
Visits Chicago on behalf of C. E. Heath

1911 Toplis and Harding (Northern) opens Manchester office
Graham Harding opens Paris office

1914 Graham Harding assessing damage in Scarborough bombardment

1917 Becomes a member of Lloyd's

1918 Visits New York and Chicago

1919 Moves business to 28 Old Jewry
Toplis and Harding (Paris) becomes Société Anonyme

1920 Opens offices in New York and San Francisco

1921 Opens offices in Alexandria, Cairo and Port Said; Constantinople and Smyrna; Montreal, Shanghai, Los Angeles; Brussels, Antwerp, Marseilles, Milan and Piraeus

1923 Toplis and Harding Inc. (Los Angeles) awarded Lloyd's Agency

1925 Toplis and Harding SA (Paris) awarded Lloyd's Agency for France

1927 Toplis and Harding Corporations in USA merge to form Toplis and Harding, Wagner and Glidden, Chicago

1933 Toplis and Harding (Northern) help solve Manchester fire-raising case
Toplis and Harding Inc. (New York) awarded Lloyd's Agency

1936 Graham Harding assesses Crystal Palace fire

1940 Fire Loss Adjusters' Association formed, with offices at Toplis and Harding, 28 Old Jewry

1944 Offices at 28 Old Jewry destroyed by V1 bomb
Re-established at 78 Cornhill

1947 Ninian Hawken returns as senior London partner

1949 Graham Harding dies in Switzerland

1950 Wyndham Harding becomes a partner

1951 Toplis and Harding Inc. (Chicago) awarded Lloyd's Agency

1956 Office opened in Baghdad
Iraq pipeline enquiry

1961 Ninian Hawken retires
Chartered Institute of Loss Adjusters formed
Hurricane 'Hattie' strikes Belize

1964 Toplis and Harding (Northern) becomes Manchester office

1966 Toplis and Harding purchase Walter Hume & Co., Dublin and Belfast

1967   Offices opened in Sheffield and Bristol
Toplis and Harding Marine founded

1970   London office moves to 10 Arthur Street

1973   Toplis and Harding KG opened with Carl Gielisch, Germany
Offices opened in Cardiff, Inverness, Birmingham, Carmarthen and Enfield

1975   Offices opened in Teheran, Kuwait, Lusaka and Hong Kong

1980   Offices opened in Aberdeen, Brighton, Haverfordwest, and Gravesend

1981   Office opened in Scunthorpe
Toplis and Harding and Partners becomes Toplis and Harding Technical

1982   Partnerships within Toplis and Harding Group bought by Resources Management Corporation (RMC) and the Sharjah Investment Corporation
Partnerships become Limited Liability Companies
Toplis and Harding (Arabia) formed

1983   Offices opened in Saudi Arabia

1986   Toplis and Harding Group sold by RMC to Abaco Investment plc

1987   Merger with Trundle, Heap and Baker
Graham Miller, Inc., acquired

1988   Wm. Elmslie & Son acquired
Toplis Elmslie Marine formed
Offices opened at Heron Quay, London Docklands
Abaco Investment becomes wholly owned subsidiary of British & Commonwealth Holdings plc
Reconstruction of the Toplis and Harding Group

1989   New Corporate Identity introduced
London head office moves to 15–21 Christopher Street

1990   Management acquisition of The Toplis and Harding Group from British & Commonwealth Holdings plc.
The Toplis and Harding Group marks its 200th Anniversary, employing over 1000 people in 143 offices worldwide.

A Note on Sources

THE EARLY history of the Toplis and Harding families may be traced in the records of the Worshipful Company of Upholders (now in the Guildhall Library of the City of London). The youthful career of James Toplis is also illuminated by that of the master to whom he was apprenticed, James Duthoit. The history of the Duthoit family is given in the *Proceedings of the Huguenot Society*, vol. 14 (1929–33), pp. 589–94. This indicates that Duthoit was born *c*.1763 and died in 1818.

The London directories of the period are useful in defining where Duthoit, and thus James Toplis, had their business. Andrews' *London Directory* for 1790 gives James Duthoit at 9 Old Broad Street, and describes him as 'upholsterer and cabinet maker'. Holden's *Triennial Directory* for 1799 gives him at the same address, as 'cabinet maker and upholder'. Kent's *Directory* for 1800 gives the same information, and indicates that he moved to 1 Budge Row in 1805. Kent's *Directory* is also the source for the various moves that James Toplis made in St Paul's Churchyard from 1810.

Other sources for later family history have been the Probate Registry (Wills), the Public Record Office, and the London Diocesan Records. Lloyd's Log has provided much assistance.

Bibliography

Brown, Antony, *Hazard Unlimited: the Story of Lloyd's of London*, 2nd edn., Peter Davies, London, 1978

Cato Carter, E. F., *Order Out of Chaos: History of the Loss Adjusting Profession*, Part I. CILA, 1984

Clayton, George, *British Insurance*, Elek, London, 1971

Crocker, William Charles, *Far from Humdrum: A Lawyer's Life*, Hutchinson, London, 1967

Crohn, H. F., *A History of Trundle, Foulkes & Co. 1933–1966* (MS, 1966)

Dearden, Harold, *The Fire Raisers*, Heinemann, 1934

Dedmon, E. *Fabulous Chicago*, Random House, New York, 1953

Dickson, P. G. M., *The Sun Insurance Office 1710–1960*, Oxford University Press, 1960

Dinsdale, W. A., *A History of Accident Insurance in Great Britain*, Stone & Cox, London, 1954

Flower, Raymond C. and Michael Wynne Jones, *Lloyd's of London, an Illustrated History*, Lloyd's, London, 1974 (revised 1981)

Hurren, George, *A History of the Phoenix Assurance Company Limited 1782–1968, and of the Pelican Life Insurance Office 1797–1907*, London, Phoenix Assurance Co., 1973

Sharp, G. T. H., *A Profession Emerges: History of the Loss Adjusting Profession*, Part II. CILA, 1986

Street, George S., *The London Assurance, 1720–1920*, privately printed, London, 1920

Supple, Barry, *The Royal Exchange Assurance*, Cambridge University Press, 1970

Trebilcock, R. C., *Phoenix Assurance and the Development of British Insurance*, vol. 1, 1782–1870, Cambridge University Press, 1985

Wilson, D. J., *100 Years of the Association of Average Adjusters*, AAA, London, 1969

Acknowledgements

I PARTICULARLY thank Mrs Angela Buckham for allowing me to reproduce the paper given by the late Donald Buckham to the Chartered Insurance Institute. I also thank Mrs Helen Marr, secretary to the late Graham Harding and then to the Chartered Institute of Loss Adjusters. For assistance in many ways I am grateful to Mr W. P. F. Bennett, Mr Ian Campbell, Mr Robert Cole, Mr J. R. Ellwood, Mr Wyndham Harding, Mr T. J. Hudson, Mr R. F. Jones, Mr M. J. Millor, Mr Roger Schwab and Mr Clive Terrill. Research on the history of Toplis and Harding was written up in the 1970s by Mr H. N. McDowall, and I have found his work a most useful signpost.

I thank Mr Drake Ratcliff of Toplis and Harding Inc. and Mr Chris Stafford of Maxson Young Associates for their contributions. At Lloyd's I thank Mr Mark Loveday, and Mr J. Curtis, Lloyd's Librarian; Mr Donald Burns of Cuthbert Heath Brokers, and Mr Geoff Shelton. Mrs Anne Ashley Cooper has kindly provided information on Hexton House (now Hexton Manor).

I thank the Sun Alliance Assurance Company for the use of their records now housed in the Guildhall Library of the City of London. Other useful sources have been the City of London Record Office, the London Library, the British Library Newspaper Library at Colindale, the Library of the Chartered Insurance Institute and of the Chartered Institute of Loss Adjusters.

I offer my apologies for any inadvertent omissions.

Index

The South Side of St Paul's Churchyard ①
From: Thomas Hornor: *Views of London*, (1822)

The first house occupied by James Toplis (in 1811) was No. 30, which is at the left-hand edge of the centre panel (the taller house with windows in pairs).

The second house occupied by 'James Toplis, Upholsterer & Co' from 1812 for some years was No. 22. This is the house with round-headed windows on the ground floor (immediately behind the lone rider on a horse). The name TOPLIS appears over the door, so clearly he was in this house in 1822.